God
and World
in Early
Christian
Theology

A Study in Justin Martyr, Irenaeus,
Tertullian, and Origen

R. A. NORRIS, Jr.

God and World in Early Christian Theology

THE SEABURY PRESS ✠ NEW YORK

TO MY PARENTS

Preface

"As though there were a *Metempsuchosis*," wrote
Sir Thomas Browne, "and the soule of one man passed into another, opinions doe finde after certaine revolutions, men and
minds like those that first begat them." This weary and perhaps
somewhat cynical observation would receive less credit nowadays
than it doubtless did in the seventeenth century. For one thing,
Browne's cyclical theory of history is no longer fashionable. At
the same time, historians have learned that there is no more certain way of distorting the past than to view it simply as a dress
rehearsal for the present, and no more certain way of misunderstanding the present than to see its problems as mere reproduc-
tions of the issues which preoccupied some past era.

We may take it, then, that the problems of modern Christian
thought have no exact parallels in the theology of the Early
Church. One cannot appeal to the past either for ready-made
solutions to contemporary questions or for precise definitions of
the questions themselves. Yet it remains true (else how—and
why—is history written at all?) that modern problems have their
analogues and, even more important, their roots in the events
and in the thought of the past.

It is with this rather diluted version of Sir Thomas Browne's
principle in mind that I have written the sketches contained in
this book. They are intended to suggest how it was that certain
early Christian writers dealt with the problem of evolving a religious world-picture which would satisfy two requirements: that
of fidelity to the teaching of the Bible, and that of consistency
with the philosophical outlook which they shared with their contemporaries. By this means, I have hoped to call attention to the

ancient analogues—and the ancient sources—of two of the central issues of contemporary theology: the question of the relation of God to the world, and (secondarily) the question of the relation between Christian teaching and "secular" thought.

These sketches are just that. They make no claim to present anything like a complete picture of the thought of the men with whom they deal. My method has been deliberately, and necessarily, selective. Neither can they claim to embody new or unheard-of material. Interested readers will find a short bibliography at the end of the book. This will assist them to find out more about the thinkers treated here, should they wish to do so. At the same time, it will supply an indication of the secondary studies to which I am principally and most extensively indebted. The bibliography is incomplete, both as a guide and as an acknowledgment; but to expand it significantly would be to give a false impression of the pretensions of the book.

I am grateful to the American Association of Theological Schools, whose award of a Faculty Fellowship for study during the summer and fall of 1964 enabled me to do the basic work for this book. I must also add a note of special gratitude to the Reverend Dr. L. G. Patterson, whose numerous suggestions and critical advice have contributed immeasurably to the substance and style of the work.

                                                      R. A. NORRIS, JR.

Table of Contents

ix

*God
and World
in Early
Christian
Theology*

Introduction

THE PHRASE "agonizing reappraisal" was coined some time ago to describe the emergence of a new phase in the history of postwar American foreign policy. But the expression is capable of a wide range of applications; and to nothing is it more appropriately applied at present than to the state of theological discussion in both Europe and America. Questions long thought of as settled are being reopened and reconsidered, and not merely by a minority of daring pioneers but by accepted leaders of the churches and even by the Christian-in-the-street. There is a feeling abroad that old patterns of thought and action are now out of place in a world that is secular minded and technologically oriented. A cultural revolution has taken place and is still continuing. Men's habits of thought—their unconscious ways of understanding the world and their life within it—are being altered substantially. Can the Church, or Christian theology, remain unaffected by these changes? Can it *afford* to remain unaffected by them? These are the questions which have stimulated the agonizing reappraisal which is even now going on in theological circles.

There are, of course, many sides to this discussion, many eddies within the prevailing current of debate, revision, and renewal. The practical, institutional relation of the Church to the society around it is one obvious focus of attention. Another is the question of the bases and content of a viable Christian ethic. But underlying these issues is another which is, logically at any

3

rate, still more fundamental. For what Christians do, collectively and individually, in the world and for it, depends upon their working idea of what the world is and of how it is related to God. That is to say, it depends upon the theological picture of the world which expresses or occasions their estimate of the meaning and direction of human life.

Such a world-picture is a complex and many-sided affair, a compound of ideas, attitudes, and hopes which in their cohesion define what might be called a "perspective" on human existence. One constituent of such a world-picture is a notion of the shape and constitution of the physical universe. Another is an idea of man, of how he is made up and of what is involved in his well-being. Closely related to these elements, and partly determined by them, is an implicit set of values: a definition of the goals and interests which make sense in a world thus envisaged. And finally, of course, there is a conception of the Divine—of powers, or values, or a reality which is supreme; and this conception is itself a correlate of the other elements in any given world-picture. That is to say, it will cohere with, just as it will in turn modify, the moral and scientific ingredients in a total view of the world.

There can be little doubt that much of the present crisis in theology is really the expression of a growing gap between the world-picture with which Christianity has traditionally worked and the typical presuppositions and attitudes of "technologized" man. So much ought to be evident merely from the interest and enthusiasm which have lately greeted the works of Dietrich Bonhoeffer and Pierre Teilhard de Chardin. These two writers, although their backgrounds, training, and experience were diverse, and their thought cast in widely differing molds, nevertheless bear joint witness in their books to the theological centrality of a single issue: that of the meaning of God and of faith in and for a universe scientifically conceived and a society secularized in its interests and attitudes. What each of them in his own way attests is the fact that traditional conceptions of the

Divine no longer appear to cohere with certain other elements in
the world-picture generated by modern Western and urban culture; and the wide impact of their opinions has undoubtedly
been encouraged by the fact that they suggest ways of rethinking
these traditional ideas. Each of them attempts in effect to provide a fresh account of God in his relation with the world, one
which will both satisfy the assumptions of modern scientific
cosmology and provide an illuminating basis for the conduct of
Christian life within the world.

It is not our purpose here to enter directly into the debate
which continues to rage around this crucial problem. It has already given rise to an extensive literature, and our intent here is
satisfied with an identification and definition of the issue. For
our particular interest lies in pointing out, if only by way of illustration, that the problem has a background and a history; that
in other times and other circumstances it has—though in significantly different form—been faced, to the accompaniment of
equally confused debate. The question of the Christian appropriation of secular scientific and philosophical ideas; the question
of making sense of the Father of Jesus Christ in terms of a
world-picture not obviously made up to fit him; the question of
interpreting Christian values and Christian hope in the light of a
not-wholly-sympathetic idea of man's nature and destiny—all
these issues have been canvassed before, most notably perhaps in
the early centuries of the Church's existence, and not without
constructive result. It may be, therefore, that some light can be
shed on the modern problem by study of its ancient analogue.

But first let us try to say more specifically what this earlier
agony of reappraisal amounted to.

In its original form, the Christian Gospel was just that: a
piece of good news, a proclamation which grew out of a particular common life and experience. Christian teachers were in the
first instance neither moralists nor philosophers nor theologians.
They were heralds of God's Messiah and his work. The Chris-

tian way was one of participation in a new life—a life which at once prepared for and anticipated the new age which the Messiah had already inaugurated and which would soon come in power. The movement thus bore plainly, in the form as well as in the content of its message, the marks of its origin within Palestinian Judaism. Those who first observed its progress appear to have thought of it as a Jewish sect; and with good reason. Its Scriptures were the Jewish Scriptures. Its message declared God's fulfillment of his promises to Israel. Its thought was stimulated by the problems which arose out of the new Church's ambiguous relation with the ancient people of God. Its teachings were formulated with reference to the traditions and thought forms of Judaism.

So in spite of its early development of a sense of world mission, this new religious movement had little obvious potentiality for widespread popular acceptance in the Roman world into which it had come. Both the message which it preached and the language which it used bore the imprint of a particular cultural, historical, and religious source. Neither the hope whose fulfillment it announced nor the conceptions which made that hope significant were shared by the vast majority of the peoples who inhabited the Mediterranean Basin. The very habits of mind which made such a proclamation meaningful were lacking to them. The Jewish origins and orientation of Christian preaching meant that it was as often as not busy supplying answers to questions which most people had never asked—as St. Paul's experience on the Hill of Mars in Athens might suggest.

Yet by the end of the third century, this situation was quite changed. Christianity, though ever bearing with it the marks of its origin, had separated from Judaism. It had in fact become a Gentile religion, with a remarkably large constituency within the Roman world. The causes and conditions of this development were manifold. Political, social, and economic circumstances, as well as prevalent religious ideals and needs, contributed to it. But one factor in the process is of crucial importance for our purposes, as indeed it was for the growth of the Church. This was the Church's development of a rational theology in the Greek tradition. There occurred a Hellenization of Christian teaching and Christian language which at once grew up in the wake of the movement and prepared the way for its further spread. Christian preachers and apologists learned to use the thought forms and the language of Hellenistic philosophy and religion. In a word, they learned to present their faith in such wise that it cohered with, as it modified, the contemporary religious and scientific world-picture.

What was involved in such an adjustment can be seen by looking at the cases of other religions of provincial origin which spread within the confines of the Roman-Hellenistic world. Christianity was by no means unique in its situation or its problem.

Alexander the Great had begun, and Augustus Caesar had in a manner completed, a historical transformation which gave to the Mediterranean world both political unity and a common intellectual culture. One result of the process of unification was that certain religions rooted in the particular cultures of individual nations moved out upon the stage of a larger world. There, these cults—"mystery religions," as they are most frequently called—were adapted to serve the religious needs of persons far removed from the experiences and patterns of life which had originally shaped the cults themselves. These national or ethnic religions in fact became Hellenized. They conformed themselves in various ways to the common culture of the Mediterranean world, a culture essentially Greek in its form.

How did such adaptation take place? It might, of course, involve in part certain purely external alterations: the assimilation of religious art forms to something approximating the best Greek taste, or the modification of barbarian excesses in ritual enthusiasm. More important than such developments as these, however, was the interpretation of the religious meaning of these cults in the light of the needs and aspirations of the city dwellers of the Hellenistic world. The advantages which the mysteries offered—a blessed immortality, freedom from the domination of cosmic powers which enslaved the soul—reflect a real and quite natural transposition of religious themes from one cultural key into another. From their almost universal origin as cults of fertility and of the underworld, these mysteries were adapted to serve the desire of Hellenistic man for an immortal life exempt from change and independent of Fate, a life supernal and divine alike in its qualities and its privileges. By this evolution, the "barbarian" cults imitated the development of the ancient Greek mysteries. But at the same time—and equally significantly—they lent themselves to rationalization in the light of current scientific and philosophical pictures of the world, of man's place in the world, and of the soul's relation with the Divine. Thus, the Hellenization of these cults involved at least two crucial elements. The first was their adaptation to serve contemporary religious needs; the second was their rational interpretation in terms drawn from a philosophical world-picture—a process which lent meaning and plausibility to their religious claims.

What was true of the mystery cults of Isis or Cybele or Dionysus was inevitably true also of Judaism in the Hellenistic world. The Judaism of the Dispersion, insofar as it was a proselytizing faith, naturally felt a pressure to make itself intelligible in terms of the religious interests and the intellectual outlook of the common Greek culture. To be sure, the faith of the Hebrew Scriptures had little in common with other religions of ethnic origin. The faith of a Jew was different both in form and in substance from the devotion of an initiate of the mysteries of Isis. Nevertheless, in the eyes of the cultured man of Hellenistic times, Judaism was bound to appear as yet another barbarian religion of great antiquity and mysterious wisdom. And what better way of appropriating this wisdom than by showing how it anticipates, complements, or corresponds with the philosophical wisdom of Greek religion?

Such a project of reinterpretation was no doubt resisted

mightily by the majority of Jews. Nevertheless, Hellenistic thought inevitably influenced Judaism; and in certain quarters the teaching of the Hebrew Scriptures was systematically transposed into the language and thought forms of Hellenistic religious philosophy. Traces of this development can be found, for example, in the Book of Wisdom. But its most typical and successful expression is to be found in the writings of Philo of Alexandria, a devout and learned Jew who was a contemporary of Christ. Philo's method is not dissimilar to that which the second-century philosopher Plutarch was to employ to explain the mysteries of Isis, or which the Stoic Cornutus would use to explain the myths of Homer and Hesiod. The results achieved by the process of reinterpretation are by no means the same in each of these cases; but there is no doubt that each writer had the same essential goal. Their idea was to show that the ancient documents, or rites, or doctrines announce in their own symbolic way truths which can be explicitly stated in terms of philosophical cosmology or ethics. Philo's particular intention seems to have been to demonstrate the superiority of the wisdom of the Old Testament by indicating how the teaching of Moses anticipates—and improves upon—that of the Greek philosophers. But the result in any case is the same: Judaism becomes a faith which can be understood and interpreted in the light of an essentially Greek religious world-picture.

When, then, we speak of a Hellenization of Christianity, we are not referring to a phenomenon which was in any way unprecedented. In its basic essentials, the problem which the early Church faced was the same as that of which Philo had been conscious. It was necessary to show how the basic principles of biblical faith could be made comprehensible in terms of the ideas and values which went together to make up the Hellenistic world-picture.

Needless to say, however, such an undertaking was a perilous one. Neither Judaism nor Christianity could be dealt with simply as a "cult." Each had an ethical and theological content of its own. To be sure, their teaching was not cast in the Greek mold. They did not proclaim, as an essential part of their doctrine, a rational world-view in which Deity figured as a principle of scientific explanation. For this reason, the affirmations of Jewish and Christian faith did not at first glance appear to contradict directly the presuppositions of Greek theological cosmology; or, to use a more exact expression, they did not appear to offer a full-blown *alternative* to that cosmology. There was, it seemed, room for adjustment; and proposals such as Philo's could look plausible even if they did not command universal agreement. On the other hand, the question of what form such an adjustment might take was not an easy one to answer. How was it possible, for example, to insinuate into a Hellenistic world-picture the notion of the absolute Lordship of God, or that of God's uniqueness and unity? Might there not be a subtle but fundamental difference of principle which made the project of Hellenization all but impossible?

Inevitably, then, the Hellenization of Christianity took the form of an extended theological debate—one which was carried on both within the Church and through a dialogue with "secular" thinkers. This debate was not without fruitful issue. On the other hand, it came, as we shall see, to no final conclusion. Indeed, if our original suggestion was correct, it is a debate which, in successively altered forms, has continued even to the present, and is reflected in current discussions of the nature of God in his relation with the world.

Our purpose, however, is to consider this debate in what might be called its original form—the form which it took in the early centuries of the Church's existence, when the ideas and doctrines which have governed Christian thinking ever since were first forged. In order to do this with any success, though, we must first have a look at the religious world-picture—the theological cosmology—which Greek science, religion, and philosophy had evolved, and which was the Christian thinker's partner, minister, and opponent in the development of a rational theology.

CHAPTER I. *Greek and Hellenistic Cosmology*

It is easy to speak carelessly, as we have done hitherto, of Hellenistic or Roman-Hellenistic "philosophy," as though in the first and second Christian centuries all the world had been agreed upon a single doctrine. There was, to be sure, a remarkable unity of outlook which prevailed in the Roman Empire at the level of popular religious philosophy and popular ethical teaching. To this extent the language we have used may be justified. Yet it would be inaccurate to say that this prevalent outlook was the expression of a unified or self-consistent philosophical point of view. It amounted, rather, to an amalgam of themes and ideas, drawn from varying sources, which in their combination gave more or less precise expression to the mood of the times, to the religious and ethical ideals, problems, and interests of the Hellenistic world. To understand this outlook, therefore, in its relation with Christian thought, it is necessary to isolate some of the elements which went to make it up; and this in turn entails a brief glance at its historical sources and development.

PHILOSOPHICAL RELIGION

In any such discussion, our attention is bound to be focused primarily on the work of philosophers. This is not

11

merely because we are most directly interested in the problems of rational theology, but also because the peculiar relation between philosophy and religion in the Greek tradition makes such a focus all but inevitable. The very growth of "religion" in the Hellenistic (and modern) sense of the word is coordinate with the rise of philosophy in Greece. In the Hellenistic world, religion (or "piety") was the expression of personal, individual dependence upon and devotion to the gods. It sprang out of a sense of personal wonder, need, and gratitude. By contrast, available literary sources suggest that in classical Greek religion such an attitude, although no doubt it existed, was not typical or widespread. Classical religion was by and large a public or family concern rather than a private affair of the individual. This is not to say, as a modern might immediately conclude, that it was insincere or merely formal. It is rather to say that the life of the community and its prosperous continuance took first place in the interests of the citizenry. The performance of religious duties— worship, by whatever acts it was expressed—was an essential and serious obligation of man as a member of a group. The problems of man the individual had yet to pre-empt the center of the religious stage. That these problems did come to dominate the scene in Hellenistic times is a fact whose explanation is unavoidably complex. But two factors at least may be mentioned.

One of these was the pattern of cultural and social changes brought about in Greece and the eastern Mediterranean as a partial consequence of the conquests of Alexander the Great. In various ways these conquests and their aftermath stimulated and assisted an alteration in the relation of the individual to the world around him. They contributed to a decline in the political importance of the city-state communities; they gave men a sense of belonging to a larger, more confused, and less secure and orderly world than the one which their forebears had known. Hellenistic man was a city dweller; but the city was no longer a world in itself, and he was conscious of a new independence and isolation. His religion, therefore, was the piety of an individual who faced the world alone in his own person; and the ancient civic religion, though it did not die by any means, no longer answered to the primary religious needs of its people.

But there is a second factor of similar importance for this development; and that, as we have suggested, is the growth of Greek philosophy itself. The philosophers contributed to it in several ways. For one thing, their questions and inquiries, even when not destructive by intent, created a psychological situation in which the individual could no longer take his religious posture simply for granted, as an uncriticized part of the life which he shared with his community. The thoughtful man became conscious of having to take personal responsibility for his religious convictions and practices. But more than this, the philosophers, in the end, produced something of a substitute for the traditional piety which their physical speculations had helped to undermine. They evolved teachings which managed to provide a focus for a piety at once critically self-conscious and rational. They speculated about the divine governance of the world. They discussed the soul, its nature, its origins, and its destiny within the universe. They sought, in the light of their evolving conception of an ordered universe, to define the human good, the "virtue" which brought well-being in its train. And in all these discussions, a certain depth of religious feeling frequently pervaded their utterances. Thus, their philosophical teaching was intended, at least in part, to furnish a religious resource for the society of their time.

How did this "philosophical religion" arise? And what were some of the forms that it took?

RATIONAL CRITICISM OF RELIGION

There seems to have been intellectual and moral criticism of the traditional religion of the Greeks from a fairly early date. This took the form of criticism of the gods of Hesiod and Homer, whose poems and myths were the literary bases of classical Greek piety. As early as the sixth century before Christ, the poet-philosopher Xenophanes launched an attack on the anthropomorphism and immorality which in his eyes marked both religious art and religious myth. He noted that both Homer and Hesiod attributed to the gods behavior and motives which all would acknowledge as scandalous if they were attributed to ordinary mortals;[1] and he pointed out how absurd it was for each race of men to portray the gods after its own image: "The Ethiopians say that their gods are snub-nosed and black; and the Thracians say that theirs are blue-eyed and red-headed." [2] Xenophanes did not leave the matter there, however. He went on to specify what seemed to him to be a worthy conception of Deity. He tried to persuade his hearers to believe that there is "One God, the greatest among gods and men, who is unlike mortals both in bodily form and thought," [3] and who is "all vision, all intelligence, all hearing." [4] Aristotle reports of Xenophanes that he taught the eternity, supremacy, and unity of God, not to mention his sphericity.[5]

From this it is easy to see that Xenophanes' purpose was not just to make sport of Homer and Hesiod. He believed that a correct grasp of the principles of nature, of the character and laws of the universal Whole, would lead to a nobler and truer idea of what the Divine really is. He wanted to substitute a rational and scientific account of Deity for the anthropomorphic myths of the classical poetry. His was the protest of the unhappy intellectual; and in the fragments of his writings which remain, the reader can detect the beginnings of a theology which is philosophical.

The kind of questionings which are found in Xenophanes did not disappear. By the time of the Athenian golden age—the era of Pericles—the extent as well as the basis of critical attacks on religion had been broadened. The public cult itself was under assault. Periclean Athens was a city in which skepticism about the traditional belief in the gods had grown, in the case of many of the intelligentsia, to the point of contempt for religious observances. Several causes contributed to this state of affairs, one of which was the effectiveness of continuing criticism of the moral character of the gods of the Homeric and Hesiodic pantheon.

Still another source of this attitude was evidently the teaching of the Sophists. These were instructors in the not-too-scrupulous arts of public argument and mass persuasion, whose teaching apparently stimulated, if it did not always directly inculcate, skepticism about conventional ethical standards. Such an attitude transferred itself easily enough from the conventions of ethics to those of religion, with the result that the gods, like the canons of social behavior, were taken by many to be mere human inventions. Various theories were propounded to explain how they came to be "made up." One man explained that they were devised to provide a supernatural sanction for moral codes; another held that they were poetic personifications of beneficent natural forces.

It is not necessary for us, however, to attempt a complete analysis of the reasons for this surge of skepticism, or to enumerate the various interpretations of religion and myth to which it gave rise. It is enough to see that the philosophical theology in which we are directly interested had its beginnings in the discrediting of traditional Greek religion; and that the causes of this development include not only the moral inadequacy of the Greek gods, but also their uselessness as principles of explanation within a universe which was conceived as a rational system. To see in what direction the currents of thought were to move, we must look at the theological world-picture of Plato—which was, perhaps, even more influential in Hellenistic times than it was in his own day or among his immediate successors.

PLATO

Plato's fundamental attitude toward the problems of his time is made plain in one of his early and inconclusive dialogues, the *Euthyphro*. The question at issue is the moral defensibility of Euthyphro's decision to prosecute his own father for the murder of a hired laborer. The traditional code of behavior laid it down that "it is unholy for a son to prosecute his father for murder." [6] Euthyphro thinks, on the contrary, that justice ought to countenance no respect of persons, not even of fathers. He appeals for his justification to the example of Zeus, who "put his father in bonds because he wickedly devoured his children." [7] Socrates in reply, however, indicates that he cannot accept such stories of the gods as credible. More than that, he cannot accept a morality based upon an appeal to the gods. For, he says, "the gods . . . quarrel and disagree with each other," [8] and thus offer neither a consistent teaching nor a worthy example. What is holy or just and what is pleasing to the gods cannot therefore be the same thing: this is Socrates' conclusion. And at the end of the dialogue, he is still searching for a rationally defensible definition of "the holy"—that is, for a publicly acceptable standard of morality.

As expressed or implied in the opinions of Socrates, Plato's attitude toward religion is ambiguous. On the one hand, he obviously shares the current disillusionment about the gods. He even doubts the meaningfulness of the public cult. [9] His point of view is made even plainer in a later dialogue, the *Republic*, in which he insists that the more pernicious and degraded myths of the poets be excluded from his curriculum for public education. Evidently, he does not think that one can turn to the ancient gods—capricious, inconsistent, and amoral, as they were conceived to be—to find the basis for an ordered life, either for the individual or for the community. No more does he think that the gods, as traditionally pictured, can be any part of that natural order of which Greek science and mathematics were becoming aware.

But on the other hand, Plato is passionately devoted to the project of finding an adequate basis in the knowable nature of things for just such an ordered communal life as the new skepticism had destroyed by its attacks on the religious foundations of the city-state. This search supplies a major part of the motive force behind his philosophical speculations. He is concerned first of all, like Socrates, to find a rational foundation for morality. But this quest leads him further, into an attempt to show that moral and social order in the human community presupposes a providential order in the universe. Hence, he elaborates in the end a scientific-religious picture of the cosmos in terms of which the meaning and goal of human life can be understood.

The first key for the understanding of Plato's elaborated world-view is his famous theory of Ideas. This theory is based upon the portentous distinction which he draws between two different kinds of reality, which he calls respectively "Becoming" and "Being." As he sees it, the world in which men live is a product of the interaction of these two principles.

By "Becoming," he intends in the first instance to denote the kind of visible, tangible reality which the senses perceive. But the real meaning of the designation only becomes clear when one sees how Plato describes and characterizes this particular kind of reality. "Becoming" is the name of an inferior sort of existence which has two essential characteristics. It is, first of all, physical or material in nature. Hence, it is made up of parts and occupies both space and time. But second, and just because its members are extended in space and time, this lower order is a world whose single universal law is that of change. Nothing in it is permanent or stable. Consequently, nothing in it quite succeeds in *being* what it is, for the good reason that it is always in process of *becoming* something else. It is, so to speak, a world which runs out between the fingers of the man who would grasp it: a world of *maybe*; *partly*, *perhaps*; and *some-*

times. And because of this, it is a world which offers in itself no basis for reliable knowledge of any kind. If a man focuses his mental energies on the flux of Becoming, he finds nothing solid or stable which the mind can grasp and on which an ordered structure of knowledge or of life can be built.

Does this mean that the search for a stable and rational order in the world is vain? Plato thinks not. In a famous image in the *Republic,* he explains that the comings and goings of things in the visible world are the flickering shadows of a reality which is more substantial. This reality is, to be sure, opaque to the senses; but a man can grasp and comprehend it by his reason, by the powers of his mind. This higher reality Plato calls "Being," and he describes it as a realm of Ideas or Forms, an *intelligible* world.

Plato was in fact much impressed by the methods and achievements of the mathematics of his day (the education which his Academy offered was fundamentally mathematical, not rhetorical or literary, in character); and he appears to have seen in mathematical understanding the model of all reliable and certain knowledge. He saw, however, that the truths of mathematics are of a special sort. They are grasped intellectually, by a process of intuition and deductive reasoning. One can see them reflected or illustrated—though only imperfectly—in the visible, physical world. But they can only be understood in their full logical rigor and absolute certainty by the mind which abstracts from the confused evidence of sense and relies on the capacities of reason alone. And as it is with the truths of mathematics, so it is, Plato thinks, with other matters as well. The "truth" of things is the immaterial Pattern which reason grasps, not the distorted and unstable shadow which the eye sees. Truth —and therefore Being—is a realm of intelligible Forms or Ideas, which are like the truths of mathematics in at least two respects. They do not change; and this means that they are eternal. Furthermore, they embody perfectly that rationality of structure and order which produces the satisfaction of complete understanding in the mind which contemplates them.

Hence, for Plato, the Ideas are "the genuinely real." They are the Truth which is changeably manifested or reflected in the order of time and space. But in themselves they are beyond time and space. Spiritual, eternal, and intelligible, they alone can be said truly to *be*. Consequently, it is to this realm that a man must turn if he seeks understanding of the natural or moral order. He must purify himself of final attachment to everything which is bodily, visible, and temporal. He must prepare himself by education and rigorous self-discipline. Then, by an ascent of the mind, he may pierce through the shifting appearances which are the world of Becoming and grasp intelligible Reality itself: that Being which stands to the inferior order as light to shadow, truth to error, clarity to confusion.

But the doctrine of Ideas, with its accompanying distinction between two different levels of reality, represents only one of the major themes in Plato's rational theology. Another, equally important for our purposes, is his use and development of the notion of "soul," an idea which is essential both to his doctrine of man and to his understanding of the natural world-order.

Plato knew two ways of employing the word "soul," both of which he adopted. One he seems to have inherited or taken over from the literature of the Orphic movement. In this use, the word denoted the unchanging interior identity of a man—immortal as distinct from the mortal body in which it was imprisoned, and divine or heavenly in its origin. The second use understood *soul* in the first instance as *life*, that is to say, as the cause or source of orderly movement. Employed in this way, the term had primarily a physical or scientific rather than a religious and moral application. Soul was appealed to as a "breath" which moves and vivifies, and which is the origin of life and motion because it is the only force which moves itself.

In the two dialogues *Phaedo* and *Phaedrus,* Plato brings

these two ideas of soul together. At the same time, he indicates where, in his view, soul stands with reference to the two orders of Being and Becoming; and in this way, his teaching about soul becomes the focal point at which his religious, moral, and scientific interests converge in a single master image.

He tries first of all to show that soul is "ingenerate and immortal," [10] that it never began to exist and will never cease to exist. To prove this thesis, he uses a number of different arguments; but one of the most prominent—and significant—of these is based on an appeal to the idea that soul is the source of all movement in the cosmos. If this is so, he contends, then the soul must be eternal, since in any other view it would be impossible to explain how the heavens maintain their eternal, orderly motion. This argument may or may not be wholly plausible; but it reveals a dimension of Plato's conception of soul which is of fundamental importance. "Soul" for him is not merely the name of a psychological or moral subject; it is also the name of a cosmic force to which he appeals for the explanation of certain universal physical phenomena. It is as the origin of harmonious movement in the visible world that the soul must be deathless and (what comes to the same thing in Greek thinking) divine.

But in Plato's view the soul's eternity both implies and presupposes a further truth about it. Once admit that it is immortal—and therefore immaterial or "spiritual"—and you cannot help seeing that in this respect it must belong in some sense to the same divine order of reality as the Ideas. And if any further proof of this were needed, it would be forthcoming in the soul's obvious and natural bent toward a contemplative knowledge of the Ideas. Only like can know like; only a subject which is itself eternal and incorporeal can grasp the truth of an eternal and incorporeal reality. If soul is energy and life, it is also *mind;* and being mind, it is true to itself only as it is formed and molded after the likeness of the unchanging truth which it knows.

Soul, then, must be envisaged in two ways at once. In Plato's dualism of material and spiritual, visible and intelligible, soul occupies a middle place and plays a mediating role. It dwells and operates in the visible world as the principle of movement and life. At the same time, however, in virtue of its capacity to know eternal truth, it is a member of the intelligible world, the realm of Being. For this reason, the motion which it imparts to the universe is *rational* motion, motion determined and guided by its apprehension of the perfect harmonies of the invisible Ideas. As the soul reaches out for and attains knowledge of Being, its own movements are so "rationalized" that it brings order to the visible world which it governs. (And would not the same be true of human society, if the souls which governed it were guided by a vision of truth?)

TIMAEUS

In one of his later dialogues, the *Timaeus*, which was probably the most widely read and influential of his writings in Roman-Hellenistic times, Plato brings all these themes together in an attempt to provide a consistent account of the structure and character of the visible world. His motives in writing this work were complex. His interests are scientific as well as moral and religious. But his primary aim—which also governs the argument of Book X of the *Laws*—is to show that the universe is not a machine or a jumble of warring energies, but an order which reflects the workings of Mind—an order in which the ultimate explanation of things is the fact that "it is best for them to be as they are." [11] Plato defends this belief by offering a religious interpretation of the geocentric cosmos which the science of his day was discovering. In the end, his philosophical effort did not achieve a reconstitution of the life of the Greek city-state, as he himself had hoped; but it did provide the theoretical basis for much of the religion of the Hellenistic era.

The *Timaeus* takes the form of a long myth of creation. It relates the steps taken by one whom Plato calls "the Demiurge" or "the Craftsman" to produce a world in whose motions and forms the beauty of the eternal Ideas will be reflected. Of course, the Craftsman is limited in what he can accomplish—not by his own intentions, but by the circumstances in which he must work. He cannot simply copy or reduplicate the intelligible world in its perfection. He has rather to reproduce its rational order in a recalcitrant medium. Consequently, as Plato is careful to point out, what he achieves is not the best absolutely, but only the best possible. What is the fruit of his work?

Plato pictures the world as a vast sphere. At its center the earth is fixed. The outer surface of the sphere is the region of the fixed stars. Between this outer surface and the center are the orbits of the seven planets. All the celestial bodies move in more or less regular circular paths, and their motion is the source and impulse for all regular motion and change within the entire system. The mathematical precision and perfect order of their movement is itself the visible, material embodiment of the unmoving perfection of the Ideas. Thus, the material world becomes, as it were, a systematically distorted image of intelligible Reality— and one whose degree of distortion increases proportionately with distance from the region of the fixed stars.

But rational and regular motion, as we have seen, implies for Plato the operation of soul. In his view, accordingly, the movement of the heavenly bodies is seen as the work of so many superior souls, beginning with the all-directing World Soul itself, which orders the motion of the circle of fixed stars, down through the Intelligences which guide the planets. These celestial souls, Plato says in the *Laws*,[12] are the gods: eternal Intellects whose knowledge of Being is reflected in the awesome, perfectly disciplined slow march of the heavens. Thus, Plato writes: "This present Universe" is "one single Living Being, containing within itself all living beings both mortal and immortal." [13]

Within this universe, man occupies a special place. He, too, is an immortal and intelligent soul, of the same family as the gods and akin to the World Soul itself.[14] Yet it is the destiny of the human soul to be sent down from the celestial world, which is its native habitat, to dwell on earth. To this end it is joined both with a body and with an inferior—mortal and irrational —soul. Under these circumstances, naturally enough, man's mind is distracted and his judgment led astray by the disordered impulses and motions of his irrational nature. However, Plato writes, if men "overcome these [passions] they will live righteously, but if they are overcome by them, unrighteously. And he who has lived well for the time appointed him will go back again to his home in his native star, and will lay hold on a life which is happy and congenial." [15] In another place, Plato explains more exactly what this means. The human soul in its immortal and rational part must, by contemplation of the perfectly harmonious revolutions of the heavenly bodies, bring its own life back into accord with the rhythms of the divine Reason's movement: it must fashion itself in the likeness of what it sees and knows, "and thereby win fulfillment of the best life set by the gods before mankind both for this present time and for the time to come." [16]

Here, then, is a mathematical astronomy, a theology, and a doctrine of salvation all worked together into one. It is not—and probably was not meant to be—perfectly coherent. Plato bills Timaeus's narrative as myth. He knows well enough that some things are better suggested than said; and he is more interested in the sense of his story as a whole than in any of its details. The essential point to grasp is that the ancient Greek nature religion has here been rationalized and sublimated: wedded at once to a new science and to a transformed Orphic idea of the origin and destiny of the soul. The *kosmos* itself, in virtue of the supreme Intelligence which indwells it, is a god. This god, however, is no capricious tyrant or arbitrary will. He is a god whose nature is made known in those unvarying mathematical regularities of motion which most fully reveal the unchanging perfection of the intelligible world of Ideas. Worship, then, is most appropriately accorded this deity—a worship inspired by a sense of beauty, and issuing in a personal contemplative appropriation of the rational order which the heavens display. This is a theology for the enlightened and educated man. With its accompanying idea of salvation, however, it is more. It is a theology which can serve as a basis for the piety of the man who seeks his eternal destiny in the realm of the gods. As such, the world-picture of the *Timaeus* was to serve Plato's posterity long and well.

But for all this, it still contains problems, ambiguities, and indecisions which were to be as important for the future as were its positive teachings.

Take, for example, Plato's account of "creation." How seriously does he mean it? To be sure, he (or Timaeus) speaks of a "Craftsman" who "makes" the world in the sense that he imposes a rational order on the chaos of Becoming; and Christians, later, were to see in this story a parallel and derivative of the narrative in Genesis. Such a notion of what is meant by "creation" is not a wholly implausible one; and Plato seems to have meant it seriously in at least one sense. He saw it, namely, as providing an analysis of the basic *principles* of the cosmic order and their interrelation. To understand the world, in this view, one must see it as the product of three factors. First, there are the Ideas, the intelligible order which provides the Pattern on which the world is modeled. Next, there is the refractory medium in which the modeling is done, what Plato vaguely explains as "necessity" or "the receptacle," and what later philosophy was to call "matter." Finally, there is the eternal Mind, whose activity realizes in the medium an image of the Pattern.

But this picture of what makes the world the sort of thing it is need not be taken as an actual account of the process by which it came into existence. Plato's description of the Craftsman's "making" the world is probably no more than a literary device. That is to say, it seems to be no more than a way of suggesting that it is appropriate to regard the world "as if" it had come into being in this fashion. Many interpreters of Plato, both ancient and modern, have argued convincingly that this is what the *Timaeus* is really meant to say. Certainly Plato denies that soul or the Ideas or even matter has any beginning of existence; and he seems to regard the world as the patterned product of their regular interaction. Why then speak of a "beginning" of the world?

But has Plato no *equivalent* for the idea of creation? This question is probably an inappropriate one to ask. The existing world, whose order he seeks to depict, is for Plato the basic *datum*. Its being there at all does not, for him, need to be explained. That can be assumed. What he is looking for is a source of stable order, moral and natural, in the world; and he finds this in the paired principles of Mind and Ideas. One can, therefore, admit that Plato's *kosmos* is in one real sense *dependent*: the visible world of Becoming is *dependent* upon Mind and the Ideas for the elements of rationality and order in its structure. But this kind of dependence is not an equivalent for an idea of "creation." It does not explain why there is a world, but what sort of thing the world is, and always has been, and always will be.

What then—and here is a second problem—does Plato understand by "god"? In principle, the answer to this query is easy enough. Plato applies the epithet "divine" to anything which participates in Being as opposed to Becoming—to anything which belongs by nature to the realm of immortal and intelligible existence. The realm of Ideas is thus pre-eminently "divine." But the same is true of all immortal intelligences: the World Soul, and even the souls of men, are "gods." Of course, they are not all divine in the same way or to the same degree. Some, so to speak, represent a pure strain; in others, there are varying admixtures of inferior stock. In any case, however, the gods include in their number all those beings whose affinity for eternal truth makes them directing powers within the universal order.

It makes very little sense, therefore, to ask whether the Plato of the *Timaeus* is a monotheist. The very manner in which he uses the word "god" makes it almost inconceivable that he should assert that there is only one being to which it may be applied. On the other hand, insofar as his sense of the unity of the cosmic order is expressed in the doctrine of a supreme Mind immanent in the world, or in the notion of a source of Being and Order beyond the visible world, one may point to this fact as making a vast difference of principle between Plato's view and what is ordinarily meant by polytheism. In the last resort, Plato identifies the divine with whatever it is that makes for harmony and rational order within the world. His thought tends, therefore, to seek a single divine principle of rational unity, whether in the world or beyond it.

This tendency is only obscurely intimated in the *Timaeus*. It comes to fuller, though still only brief, expression in a passage in the *Republic*, in which Plato refers to what he calls "the Idea of the Good." [17] This he seems to understand as the highest—and therefore most divine—principle of all, that perfect Unity which is first articulated in the rational system of Ideas and then expressed in the motions and order of the visible world. As such, it is not to be identified with what Plato has called "Being," that is, the intelligible world. It is "beyond Being," because it is the source of Being and intelligibility. This means, however, that it cannot be understood or grasped by the mind. In its unity and simplicity, it is accessible only to a kind of mystical experience. The Idea of the Good thus stands, in Plato's system, for a limit to the mind's search for rational order and stability in a changing world. It is the point at which all things may be seen as one, and the point whence all order flows. Later philosophy and theology were, as we shall see, to make a great deal of this conception of an incomprehensible Absolute. Plato himself, however, does no more than make mysterious mention of it. It was left for future thinkers to develop its implications.

It should be clear by now that when the Hellenistic world inherited Plato's "new theology," it took over a system whose exact meaning was not absolutely obvious. What were its implications for piety? Is the goal of worship to rise from contemplation of the visible heavens to contemplation of the intelligible world which their movements reflect? And is the Idea of the Good—the source of that light which plays over the Ideas—the supreme objective of the religious search? Or does the *kosmos,* the World Soul embodied, deserve worship in its own right? Perhaps Plato meant all these things. But he is not wholly clear; and Hellenistic piety tended to move back and forth between worship of the *kosmos,* the heavens, and worship of a supramundane Divinity.

Yet on one matter Plato's meaning was quite plain. The soul of man is akin to whatever in the world-order is divine and immortal. Its *true* home is with the gods; and its true destiny is to delight in the contemplative knowledge of Being. It was this part of Plato's teaching which most obviously influenced the piety of later times; and with it went, in one form or another, the ideas which gave it point: the contrast between the two orders of Being and Becoming, the conviction that man realizes himself fully only as he turns away from absorption in the affairs of the physical world and attends inwardly to a reality which only the mind can grasp. These ideas were to become, in ever changing forms, part of the common religious heritage of the world into which Christianity came.

THE STOICS

But not immediately. Plato's "new theology," the world-picture of the *Timaeus,* had serious rivals; and until, roughly speaking, the first century before Christ, the rivals held the field. Plato's own followers in the Academy tended to be more interested in the logical than in the moral and religious aspects of his work. His pupil Aristotle founded a new school whose concerns were primarily scientific, and whose ethical and religious teaching offered in any case a significant contrast to

Plato's. Needless to say, however, his ideas were not without influence even on his critics. In radically altered form, the world-picture of the *Timaeus* did manage to survive; and interestingly enough, it did so most clearly in the teaching of the most influential of the Hellenistic schools, that of the Stoics.

Indeed, from one point of view, the most striking fact about the Stoic world-picture was its resemblance to Plato's. The Stoics, too, portrayed the *kosmos* as a great Animal: an ensouled and therefore living organism. They saw the world as the product of two interacting principles, the one active and determinant, the other passive and determined. The first they called "spirit" or "breath," the second they called "matter"; and they conceived the relation between these on the analogy of the relation of soul and body. Spirit, they taught, penetrates and pervades the whole of the universal body. At various levels of operation, it functions as the cohesive force in inanimate bodies, the power of life in plants and animals, and the reason in man. In its highest and essential nature, however, it is the divine Reason (*Logos*), called also Zeus, or Fate, or God, which binds the whole world into one integrated system, and predetermines all events according to a providential order.

But if this picture of the world is similar to Plato's in its general outlines, it differs vastly from his in other fundamental respects. For one thing, the Stoics, like their Epicurean contemporaries, were materialists. For them, both spirit and matter were *bodies,* and their relations were conceived to be of a physical order. Thus, they described the World Soul as composed of a fine, fiery substance, capable of penetrating completely the coarser substance of the world's body; and they applied the same description to the soul of man, which they understood to be a "spark" or fragment of the divine Reason.

In such a materialistic system, there was no room for Plato's idea of a transcendent intelligible world. The dualism which had led Plato to base his thought on the contrast between Being and Becoming, physical and nonphysical orders of reality, completely disappears. For the Stoics the visible world is self-contained and self-renewing. One need not look beyond it to find its principle of order and cohesion. Hence, there was no confusion in Stoic circles as to the meaning of "god." The Divine was, for them, simply the immanent rational Power which guides and governs the world, and of which the soul of man is a portion. Plato feels a compulsion to look beyond the world for an explanation of its order; not so the Stoic.

And, of course, these differences are reflected in a further difference of religious and ethical teaching. The Stoic sage could not seek his destiny in a release or escape from the bondage of his embodied earthly existence, or in the contemplation of a spiritual reality beyond the visible world-order. He agreed with Plato that man's highest calling is to realize his fellowship, his oneness, with the Divine. But in the case of the Stoic, this meant the achievement of an interior conformity of will and thought with the divine Reason which governs the course of the world. Such conformity he called "the life according to Nature," and he identified it with virtue, which in turn he regarded not as the way to happiness but as happiness itself. This doctrine inculcated an attitude of noble indifference to exterior circumstance. It taught that man's happiness was purely a matter of moral character, and that affairs over which the human will had no control—good and ill material fortune, the occasions of normal joy and sorrow—were therefore irrelevant to his well-being. The Stoic could not hope, as could the follower of Plato, that the soul might escape the "changes and chances of this mortal life." Therefore, he sought his happiness in a posture of unruffled impassivity, which was rooted in an interior assurance of his union with the divine Reason.

Such nobility of attitude, however, was not within the reach of many. Stoic determinism, which on the one hand produced the high-minded ethic of virtue for virtue's sake, on the other hand stimulated the ordinary man's sense of helplessness and oppression before the world-system. It joined with astrological doctrines and with ideas of the rule of Fate or Fortune to encourage a feeling that the terrestrial world is a kind of closed prison house in which the life of man is subjected to the domination of forces beyond his control. For just this reason, it assisted in generating a desire for a kind of salvation which Stoicism in its original form could not offer.

The mystery religions, of course, responded to this sort of need. But a theological world-picture which could also assist in meeting it was only provided with the revival—initially within Stoic circles—of the Platonism of the *Phaedo* and the *Timaeus*. This revival, beginning in the first century before Christ, gave rise to a new intellectual movement, loosely knit and highly diversified, which mingled together in varying proportions elements of Platonic, Stoic, and Aristotelian philosophy, theology, and ethics. Ultimately, in the third Christian century, this movement produced in Neoplatonism a new religious and philosophical synthesis. But we must bend our attention upon two earlier examples of its thought, both of which are roughly contemporary with the beginnings of a Christian rational theology.

DE MUNDO

The first example is the interesting treatise *De mundo* ("On the World"), which was traditionally, though falsely, attributed to Aristotle. This book was probably written in the first or second Christian century. The man who wrote it was basically a Stoic in his outlook; but what makes the work notable is the way in which it employs partially disguised Platonic ideas. As the title suggests, the treatise is a scientific account of the structure and constitution of the universe; but this account includes, as we might expect, a theology.

By "world" or *kosmos* is meant, of course, the system of stars and planets which, in the enduring spirit of "cosmic piety," is portrayed as the noblest and highest reality, alone worthy of wonder, and only to be comprehended by the philosophically disciplined intellect. As for Plato earlier, the earth is regarded as the center of this system. "The upper portion of the universe has fixed bounds on every side, the highest part of it being called heaven, the abode of the gods." [18] This highest part of the world is also the noblest, being composed not of one of the four elements, but of a fifth "indestructible and divine" [19] stuff, the ether. This is the natural home of immortal beings, just as the lowest region, earth, as well as the three intervening regions of fire, air, and water, is the home of mortal beings.

All these contrary elements are blended together in relations of harmony and proportion by "the world's noblest part," [20] the "cause which holds all things together." As in Stoicism, then, the God of the *De mundo* is an immanent cohesive force as well as a directing Reason. He is within the world, not outside it or above it. Nevertheless, he is *localized* within it. The writer does not agree with the saying that "All things are full of God." [21] On the contrary, he insists, God has

obtained the first and highest place and is therefore called Supreme, and has, in the words of the poet,

Taken his seat in heaven's topmost height;

and the heavenly body which is nearest to him most enjoys his power, and afterwards the next nearest, and so on successively until the regions wherein we dwell are reached. Wherefore the earth and the things upon the earth, being farthest removed from the benefit which proceeds from God, seem feeble and incoherent and full of much confusion . . . [22]

Described further as "Ruler and Father of all things," this God is not visible to the physical eye, but only to the reason, which sees his power reflected in his works and knows him to be "in might . . . most powerful, in beauty most fair, in time immortal, in virtue supreme." [23] "Enthroned amid the immutable," [24] he is the pilot of the cosmic ship, the keystone of the cosmic arch, many-named and immortal.

In this remarkable account, which doubtless reflects a widespread popular attitude, it is easy to see a subtle and not-wholly-unconscious interweaving of Stoic and Platonic ideas. The picture is that of a self-contained universe. There is not a hint of any divine principle apart from the cosmic God—a God who is in fact the organizing force of the natural order, himself conceived in quasi-physical terms. Theology is still essentially physics or astronomy studied with a sense of awe, and the philosopher's proper worship is still the contemplation of the marvels of the natural order.

Yet the writer reveals a preoccupation with other than scientific and intellectual issues. He wants to explain the troubled and confused character of earthly life; that is, he is concerned, as Plato had been in his own way, with the problem of evil. And like Plato again, he tries to solve this problem by importing into his world-order a dualism, which comes to light in two ways. It manifests itself in one fashion in the emphasis placed on the sheer physical distance between heaven and earth, and on the consequent absence of a *direct* divine governance of earthly affairs. Thus, the writer deviates from Stoicism by stating a doctrine of divine transcendence. But what this means to him is not that God is beyond the world-order, but that within the world, and as a part of it, he is spatially removed from its lower regions.

Then, second, the author applies to this world-scheme of his a terminology which reflects (though it does not reproduce) Plato's distinction between Being and Becoming. Heaven, he says, is the realm of the immortal, invisible, and unchanging; in the lower regions, change and mortality prevail. Thus, what for Plato was in principle a distinction between two orders of existence, here becomes merely a distinction between the characteristic qualities of life in two different regions of the world.

But it is easy to see how this cosmic geography could be given a very practical religious meaning, quite apart from its significance for the philosopher's intellectual worship. For in this scheme it becomes meaningful, as it was not in classical Stoicism, to speculate about the immortality of the soul, and to wonder whether there is not a hope of salvation for man in the transference of his home from earth to heaven. The *De mundo* comes much closer than earlier Stoicism to a full appropriation of the religious sense of the *Timaeus*.

EPITOME OF THE TEACHINGS OF PLATO

But the revival of Platonic thought and theology during the first centuries of the Christian era did not show itself merely in modifications of Stoicism. In the movement which historians have called "Middle Platonism," there appeared a group of teachers who made it their business simply to expound Plato's thought. In the process of interpreting him, they inevitably revised and modified some of his ideas, usually under the influence of Stoic or Aristotelian doctrines, which they "read into" his dialogues. The result, however, was a series of systems which are recognizably Platonist, even if they are not strictly Platonic. We can study a fairly typical example of such a system in the philosopher Albinus's *Epitome of the Teachings of Plato,* which in addition to sections on logic and ethics, contains a treatment of the problems of theology and cosmology based explicitly on the *Timaeus*. The *Epitome*, written in the second Christian century, has the additional advantage of being a textbook; so that one may assume that its ideas reflect fairly widespread opinions.

Albinus holds—and this means that he thinks Plato also held—that the world is eternal. Hence, he offers no teaching about a temporal origin or "creation" of the world. Like Plato, however, he offers an account of the various factors which together explain how the world is made up. He explicitly assumes the validity of Plato's distinction between the two orders of Being and Becoming: the one intelligible, immaterial, unchanging; the other visible, material, an endless procession of birth and decay. In Albinus's language, these are the orders of the "ingenerate," or "unbegotten," and of the "generate," or "begotten." To the former belong all intelligences or rational souls; to the latter, the physical world in all its parts. Furthermore, Albinus assumes that the generate world is dependent upon the ingenerate—not, of course, for its existence, but for its rational organization and articulation.

How this is so becomes clear when Albinus turns to his direct teaching about the *archai:* the "beginnings" or principles or ultimate determinants of the world-order. These turn out to be the same as those suggested by Plato in the *Timaeus:* the model, the modeler, and the medium, or (in Albinus's terminology) the Ideas, God, and Matter. No account is given of the origin of any of these three. They are "firsts"; and Albinus's teaching is concerned simply with the question of their enduring relations with one another.

A closer look at what Albinus says shows at least two important differences between what Plato seems to have taught and what his disciple represents him as teaching. This is most obvious in the case of the Ideas. For Plato the Ideas were in themselves a separate intelligible world beyond the visible universe. For Albinus, on the contrary, they are eternal and changeless thoughts in the mind of the supreme God. And this significant alteration in the status of the Ideas points directly to a second and even more basic difference with Plato. Albinus explicitly asserts the existence of a "First God" who transcends the world. It is doubtful whether Plato ever seriously considered such an idea. Nevertheless, it was suggested to Albinus, or to his teachers, by certain passages in the Master's writings: those, namely, in which the mythical Craftsman is mentioned, and the mysterious section of the *Republic* in which Plato speaks of the Idea of the Good. It also seems to be the case that Albinus was influenced in this interpretation of Plato by Aristotle's notion of an unmoved First Mover.

How does Albinus characterize this First God? He describes him as a divine Intelligence who is the ultimate, unchanging source of all motion and order, the apex of ingenerate existence. The World Soul of the *Timaeus* is not forgotten. But in this scheme he is an inferior, secondary deity who mediates between the First God and the world. The supreme God himself is no definable part or aspect of the world-system. But, although he is not a particular force within the world, like the God of the *De mundo,* neither is he a reality separable from it. He is known through his being essentially different from the world-order, which he explains. Thus, he fits into none of the categories of human thought. This God

is ineffable and can be grasped only by the intellect . . . since he is neither genus nor species nor difference. No more can any accidental characteristic be ascribed to him: not evil . . . nor good . . . nor quality . . . nor absence of quality. He is not a part of anything nor a thing which possesses parts. He is not the same as anything, nor is he different from anything; for nothing is said of him which can separate him from other things. He does not move and he is not moved.[25]

He is the final source and presupposition of being, intelligibility, and order; and because this is so, he cannot simply be identified with any of these things.

With this doctrine, Middle Platonism makes explicit a tendency of thought which we have seen to be native to the Platonic tradition. At the same time, it adds a new dimension to the world-picture of the Greeks. The cosmic theology which in variant forms we have seen in the *Timaeus,* in Stoicism, and in the treatise *De mundo* is retained in Albinus. Also retained is Plato's suggestion that the mind in its search for ultimate truth must pierce behind the divine *kosmos* to the intelligible world, which it mirrors. But Albinus (and not Albinus alone) finds in the tradition which he has received the suggestion of yet another stage in the mind's search, a final rung on the ladder which leads from the confusion and disorder of generate existence to the supreme reality of ingenerate Being. This is that Divinity which, he remarks paradoxically, is grasped by the mind even though its nature is inexpressible: that Divinity which, he says echoing Plato, is to the intelligible world what the sun is to the visible world, the blinding source of light.

In this theology, as in all the systems at which we have glanced, there is thus marked out a way which man can follow. It is in the first instance a way for the mind, a path to be traversed if one is to arrive at an understanding of that stable reality which is the rational order of things, the comprehensible "sense" which the world makes. To call later Greek theology a "rational theology" is to direct attention to just this aspect of its enterprise. It seeks the ultimate principle of order in a world whose orderliness is not always apparent. But the intellectual search for a single reason of things is also the soul's religious search for its true home: a search which calls it away from absorption in the transient and particular to a life which shares in as it contemplates the reality of what is ultimate, permanent, and universal.

To be sure, there were varying estimates of the character of this final reality, just as there were corresponding variations in people's views of the practical steps which must be taken if a man is to realize his unity with the ultimate. The Platonist turns from the visible and material order. As immortal soul, he flees the irrationalities, distractions, and disorders of embodied life in order to realize his kinship with a world beyond time and change and passion. The Stoic has no such hope. His freedom from passion and disorder lies in his interior assent to the divine Reason which governs the world, and in his consequent indifference to external circumstance. But despite these differences, the logic of the common quest remains the same. The religious quest for individual salvation is wedded to a rational inquiry into the character and structure of the world. In both systems, a rational and scientific view has replaced a mythological account of nature. In both, "God" is the name of the explanation of natural order.

CONCLUSION

Now whatever else one may wish to say about the teaching of the primitive Christian Church, it is clear that its proclamation did not take shape among people who thought in terms of the Greek world-picture whose outlines we have been tracing here. The differences between the two outlooks may not be immediately apparent to someone who lives in the twentieth century. Such a man is, after all, the heir of the wedding of these two streams of thought. But the differences are real and fundamental. They do not spring from variations of opinion on this or that point of doctrine. They grow out of different interests, preoccupations, and methods of thought. What this means can be seen if we look for just a moment at the ways in which Jewish-Christian writers normally use the two crucial ideas of "God" and "world," and contrast them with what we have seen of Greek usage of the same words.

Take "world" first. To the Greek from the time of the first philosophers on, this word, as we have seen, meant basically a *natural order*: a system of universal relations which constitutes the framework of human life. First of all, it denotes the system of the heavens themselves, where the orderliness and beauty of nature is most fully revealed. And it implies an *eternal* order, one which, for practical purposes, does not change in its structural character, even though the things and events in which this order is realized are in constant process of alteration.

What now of "world" in the tradition of the Hebrew Scriptures and of Christian preaching? Here the focus of attention is quite different. The world is now the complex tapestry of human life and human decision, viewed in historical perspective and evaluated in terms of its correspondence with a divine will which inexorably seeks the fulfillment of its purposes. This world is not an eternal order. It has a past different from its present; and it will have a future different from both. The critical

junctures in this world, the articulations of its structure, are not
the enduring relations of its constituent principles, but times of
transition and judgment which mark alterations in the meaning
or quality of human life. The world of nature is not forgotten.
But neither is it the center of interest. It is like the stage setting
for a drama: subordinate both to the actors and their movements
and to the purposes of the author or producer. It finds its meaning in the developing story for which it provides a setting.

And much the same sort of contrast emerges if we consider
the use of the word "God" in the two traditions. For the Greek,
as we have in effect seen, this word is the name of a *kind* of
thing: a kind of existence characterized by rationality, perma-
nence, and stability. It may therefore be applied correctly to a
number of different beings. Insofar as the world of which these
divinities are the primary forces or principles is *one* world, it is
quite natural to speak of a single supreme God, who then becomes the head of a hierarchy of deity. It remains, however, that
Greek theology tends to use the term "God" to refer to a universal principle of explanation, a presupposition of the world-order
viewed as a natural system.

The Hebrew Scriptures know such a use of the word "God,"
though in a much less sophisticated form than that in which it
characterizes the theology of the Greeks. The elements of a primitive nature religion inform the background of Hebrew, as they
do of Greek, religious thought. But whereas the Greeks transformed a primitive nature religion into a rational theology of
nature, the Hebrews transmuted a similar nature religion into a
theology of historical experience. In the tradition which the
Christian Church inherited from Israel, "God" is not used to
denote a *kind* of thing, but to name that specific will whose purposes were detected in the critical events of Israel's history and
of world history. Neither, therefore, does the word in the first
instance denote a principle of universal explanation: that is to
say, an explanation of the uniformities and regularities of the
course of nature. Rather it denotes the purpose discerned in

events or persons which depart from the ordinary and are acknowledged as in some sense special or exceptional. The Greek deity is the final point of stability in a world of apparently senseless change. The Hebrew Lord is the initiator of significant change which transforms the character of historical experience. As such, he, like the events through which he is known, has a specific character. Hence, in the first instance he is named, not defined; and as the Lord of world history he is unique.

More could be said to spell out these contrasts further. But we are interested not in the contrast itself, but in the process by which Christian teachers minimized or, perhaps, overcame it in their attempts to interpret the meaning of the Christian message to a society whose understanding of God and man grew out of a Greek world-picture.

Notes to Chapter I

1. Diels-Kranz, *Fragmente der Vorsokratiker*, I, 132.
2. *Ibid.* 133.
3. *Ibid.* 135.
4. *Ibid.*
5. *De Xenophane* I.
6. *Euthyphro* 4 E (tr. Fowler).
7. *Ibid.* 6 A.
8. *Ibid.* 7 B.
9. *Ibid.* 14 E.
10. *Phaedrus* 246 A.
11. *Phaedo* 98 A.
12. *Laws* X, 899 B ff.
13. *Timaeus* 69 C (tr. Bury); cf. 30 D.
14. Cf. *Timaeus* 41 A ff.
15. *Timaeus* 42 B (my translation).
16. *Ibid.* 90 B (tr. Cornford).
17. Cf. *Republic* 507 B–509 B.
18. *De mundo* 391 b 14 f. (tr. Forster).
19. *Ibid.* 392 a 9.
20. *Ibid.* 397 b 12 f. (Forster's translation revised).
21. *Ibid.* 397 b 16.
22. *Ibid.* 397 b 24 ff. (Forster's translation revised). The text quotes *Iliad* I.499 etc.
23. *De mundo* 399 b 20 ff.
24. *Ibid.* 400 b 11.
25. *Epitome* X.3 (my translation).

CHAPTER II. *Justin Martyr and Platonism*

IT IS impossible to specify a definite point of time, or to identify a particular writing, which marks in a clear way the beginning of what we have called the "dialogue" between Greek theology and the tradition of Christian teaching. Indeed, as we have seen, there is a sense in which the Church did not so much initiate this dialogue as inherit it. The use of Greek ideas for the interpretation of the Hebrew Scriptures had begun before the appearance of Christianity, in the Judaism of the Hellenistic Dispersion. The translation of the Law and the Prophets into the Greek tongue was the first notable step in a process which reached its culmination in the exegetical writings of Philo of Alexandria. The Bible which the early Church used was thus already a Greek Bible, and by the time of the Apostles there existed a persuasive model for its interpretation by means of Greek philosophical and ethical conceptions. For this reason, it is better to say that Christians entered into a conversation which had been going on in one form before they came upon the scene.

It is not surprising, therefore, to find that individual ideas and forms of language which derive ultimately from Greek theology and philosophy are present in Christian writings of the first and early second centuries. This is true of certain documents later included in the New Testament, just as it is of the writings

41

of the so-called Apostolic Fathers. What it marks, however, is not, at this stage, a conscious dialogue with Greek thought or Greek thinkers. Rather, it marks the Church's natural, instinctive, and unsystematic appropriation of certain of the intellectual resources of Hellenistic culture and of Hellenistic Judaism in particular.

But if it is true that the beginnings of our dialogue cannot be marked out clearly and unmistakably, it is also true that one can discern a point in the history of the early Church at which the conversation became direct and conscious, and the more or less unthinking appropriation of helpful ideas gave way to a critical attempt to show what Christian teaching meant when it was understood in the light of the questions which Greek theology had tried to answer. Most historians would locate this point in the period just following the middle of the second century, from which there have been preserved the writings of a number of Christian authors who are collectively called the Apologists. The members of this group do not by any means share a single point of view; nor are their writings to be classified as belonging to a single literary type. They do, however, have one thing in common, and that is their absorption in the problems of the relation of Christianity to the pagan world which surrounded it.

Most frequently, of course, the Apologists are remembered for their protests against the persecutions which were visited upon the churches by the Roman state. But this political and social problem represents only one focus of their interest. Of equal importance to them—and of more importance to us—is their concern to explain and defend the content of Christian teaching in the face of attack and misunderstanding.

In this connection, the Apologists found themselves with two jobs on their hands. They were obliged to expound certain distinctive points of Christian teaching in a way that would make their meaning clear to people whose habits of thought raised a barrier to understanding. But at the same time, as they attempted this, they were bound to indicate both how Christian teaching differed from other points of view, current or traditional, and how it was superior to them. In the course of this enterprise, they made much—inevitably—of the contrast between Christian monotheism and the crude polytheism of the classical Greek and barbarian mythologies. This was a natural and an easy undertaking, for which there was an abundance of ammunition ready to hand. They could draw not only on the resources of the traditional Jewish polemic against polytheism but also on those of Greek criticism of the Homeric and Hesiodic mythologies. But they could not stop at this point. Their enterprise also compelled them to take seriously the claims of Greek philosophical theology—both as a framework of thought within which their own ideas could be explained, and as a rival "system" whose defects had to be exposed.

From the beginning, therefore, the attitude of Christian writers toward Greek theology was ambiguous. Its ideas and methods played two distinct roles in their thought. On the one hand, they saw it, for the most part unconsciously, as the normal way of thinking about God and the world: that is, as a theological idiom whose logic was appropriate to the set of problems with which they were coming to grips. On the other hand, they saw it as a body of specific teachings which had to be accepted or rejected on their merits; and in this guise it was, for the most part, treated as dangerous at best. The simultaneous receptivity and hostility of the Apologists—and of later Christian writers as well—to Greek theology can only be understood when this distinction between its two roles is kept in mind. The paradox, if it is a paradox, is nicely illustrated in the writings of Justin Martyr, one of the most influential of the Apologists, and the earliest of whose writings we have any substantial remains.

JUSTIN AND HIS CONVERSION

In his *First Apology*, addressed to the Emperor Antoninus Pius, Justin describes himself as "son of Priscus the son of Bacchius, who came from Flavia Neapolis in Palestine, in the Province of Syria." [1] His Palestinian origins, however, should not be taken as evidence that Justin was of Semitic stock. Quite apart from the names of his father and grandfather, which carry no suggestion of native Palestinian derivation, there is the indication supplied by the note of his birthplace. Flavia Neapolis, the modern Nablus, was near the site of the ancient Shechem, but was the foundation of the Emperor Vespasian, who peopled it with Greek and Roman colonists. It is more than probable, therefore, that Justin was of Gentile stock and that his education was of the ordinary sort for a pagan boy of his time.

Not a great deal is known about Justin's later career. He was a Christian by conversion, not by upbringing; and there is a possibility that his conversion took place at Ephesus, where he seems to have lived for a time. The church historian Eusebius records that Justin lived at Rome,[2] and that there, "in the dress of a philosopher," [3] he taught Christian doctrine. It was at Rome also, during a second stay,[4] that Justin was martyred for his faith. His testimony at his trial before Rusticus, the Prefect of Rome, suggests that he was a sort of Christian intellectual who taught the doctrines of Christianity in much the same way as other philosophical preachers of the time taught those of the Cynics or Stoics.[5]

Eusebius also suggests that Justin was a fairly prolific author. Of his works, however, only three have been preserved. Two of these are apologies, addressed to the Roman authorities in the interest of the Christians. The third is the well-known *Dialogue with Trypho,* in which Justin engages in lengthy argument with a friendly but unconvinced Jew. This work is invaluable not only for the light which it sheds on early Christian exegesis of the Jewish Scriptures but also for the section of intellectual autobiography which leads up to Justin's account of his conversion.[6] In this section, Justin relates the history of his attempts to find a reliable philosophical guide, and its culmination in his discovery of the unfamiliar wisdom of the Old Testament prophets and the Christ whom they had foretold.

This intellectual autobiography is, all things considered, a curious and puzzling document. It is not easy to decide just how far Justin is recording the sober facts of his own experience, and how far he is idealizing his experience to bring it into accord with a not uncommon literary convention of his time, which he uses to make a polemical point. In all probability, the second alternative is the correct one. Justin adapts to his purposes a commonplace form of satire on the quirks and inadequacies of the current philosophical schools, which he then caps with an account of his meeting with the true wisdom in the form of Christianity. But even though his story may not be trustworthy as a piece of straightforward autobiography, it nevertheless casts a great deal of light on Justin's intellectual outlook, his equipment as a philosopher, and his view of the relation between Christianity and Greek philosophy.

The account begins with a brief encomium on philosophy, "the love of wisdom," which Justin defines as the search for God.[7] This is immediately followed, however, by a complaint about the division of philosophy into warring sects and schools. Justin asserts that originally philosophy was "sent down" to men;[8] by which he presumably means that it was in some way divinely revealed. Now, however, its primitive unity and purity have been corrupted by the vanity and laziness of the men who handed it on from generation to generation, with the result that it is, as he phrases it, "many-headed." To establish clearly the absurdity and iniquity of this state of affairs, Justin narrates his own experiences in the pursuit of philosophical truth. These, he thinks, yield a convincing illustration of his thesis that philosophy has fallen on evil days, and that Trypho would profit more by giving his undivided attention to Moses and the prophets than by following the way of the philosophers.

He relates that his introduction to philosophy came when he entered the school of a Stoic master. But this Stoic neither offered nor sought a knowledge of God, and Justin therefore left him, to turn to a disciple of Aristotle. The Peripatetic, how-

ever, lived up too well to the reputation of his sect for being a
school of moneygrubbers; and when he demanded payment in
advance for his lessons, Justin again moved on. This time he
sought out a well-known Pythagorean, but left him also when he
turned out to be more concerned with academic preliminaries
than with the true object of philosophy. It was at this point that
Justin turned to the Platonists—who, as recent scholarship has
made clear, were representative of some such point of view as
Albinus's.

On the subject of the Platonists, Justin is less severe. With
them, as he confesses, he made progress, though a growth in vanity accompanied his advance in knowledge. He achieved an intellectual grasp of immaterial realities: "the contemplation of the
Ideas," he writes, "made my mind take flight," [9] and he allowed
himself to hope—stupidly, as he observes—that he would come
forthwith to the vision of God. But whatever may be his distaste
for the pretentiousness which he learned at the feet of his Platonist teachers, he obviously thinks that they pointed him in the
right direction, even though they could not finally show him the
truth which he sought.

The nature of Justin's sympathy with the Platonists is
clarified as he continues his narrative and explains his conversion
to Christianity. This took place, he tells us, as the result of a
seaside conversation with an unnamed and mysterious old man.
The old man revealed to Justin certain fallacies and omissions
in the teaching of the Platonic schools—faults which, as Justin
indicates, can in part be corrected by a more careful interpretation of the *Timaeus*.

To some of the details of these criticisms we shall allude
later. At the moment, what must concern us is the general drift
or purpose of the old man's argument—which is simply to show
that the knowledge of God, the admitted objective of philosophy,
is not available to the mind which is "uninstructed by the Holy
Spirit." [10] It is of no use, the old man insists, for Justin to turn to
philosophy for enlightenment. The philosophers cannot offer
what they do not possess. If he seeks the knowledge of God, he

must seek it at the hands of men who have been taught by God: that is, the inspired prophets of the Jewish Scriptures, "who both gave glory to the Maker of all things . . . and announced the Messiah whom he sent, his Son." [11]

Justin relates that at the end of this conversation, the old man disappeared. "But immediately a fire sprang up in my soul. I was possessed by a longing for the prophets and for those men who are friends of Christ. And as I turned over his words in my mind, I discovered that this philosophy alone is trustworthy and profitable. It is in this sense and for this reason that I am a philosopher." [12] In short, Justin found in Christianity the end of man's philosophical search for "the knowledge of Reality and a clear understanding of Truth." [13]

In the past, some interpreters of Justin have placed great emphasis upon his description of Christianity in this passage as a "philosophy." They have argued that it provides an essential clue to his theological outlook, which was that of a man who sees in the Christian Gospel a speculative system of thought, rather than a proclamation of God's forgiveness or an announcement of his moral will. Whether such an interpretation of Justin's thought is in the last analysis correct, it is impossible to say here. But it should be clear that it reads rather too much into his narrative in the *Dialogue*. For him, it should be clear, philosophy is not so much "speculation" as it is a religious search for the vision of God. Justin shared this view of the nature of philosophy with most of his contemporaries. If, then, Christianity is a "philosophy," this is not to say that it is primarily a set of speculative ideas, but that it offers in reality what philosophy only promises: the bringing together of man with God. But even this fact, as Justin recognizes, does not mean that Christianity is the same sort of thing as philosophy, since what it offers proceeds not from the innate capacities of the mind, but from the gift of God. Justin calls Christianity a "philosophy" in much the same sense as that in which a psychoanalyst might refer to his couch as a "confessional."

But Justin's observation does imply some relation between

Christian belief and Greek philosophy; and his obvious indebtedness to philosophical sources for much of his language and many of his ideas suggests that he would not dismiss the rational theology of the Greeks as simply profitless and false. Does Justin then have a general theory about the relation of Christian teaching to Greek theology? And how does this theory work itself out in his own theological practice? The answers to these two questions will supply the basic outlines of an answer to our general question about his adaption of Christian doctrines to a Greek religious world-picture.

JUSTIN ON PAGAN PHILOSOPHY

The first of our questions concerns, in effect, Justin's view of the status, the origins, and the uses of Greek philosophy. To it he returns not one answer, but three different answers whose relations one to the other are far from clear. Nevertheless, the over-all sense of his teaching on this subject is plain enough; and it amounts to a definition of a Christian attitude toward the "secular" learning of the second century.

One of his explanations we have already encountered. It occurs at the beginning of Justin's autobiographical discourse, where he contrasts the primitive with the present state of philosophy. In this account he characterizes the philosophy of his day as the degenerate issue of an original revelation, which was made (or so his language suggests) to a group of men, rather than to a single individual. More than this it is difficult to say, since Justin does not discuss this theory in any other passage of his extant works. It is likely enough that his presentation of it is motivated by its appropriateness to the particular train of thought he is following in this section of the *Dialogue,* and that he is not concerned either to work it out in detail or to survey its broader implications.

Nevertheless, the argument—which has parallels in non-

Christian writings—expresses an attitude which is authentically Justin's. It seems to him not merely that the philosophical quest has a noble and a valid goal, but also that the teachings of the philosophers contain undeniable truths and valuable insights. Thus, he approves of certain elements in the teachings of Plato and the Stoics; and he praises Socrates as one who tried, by an appeal to reason, to deliver his fellows from the service of demons—a judgment which makes of Socrates a precursor of the work of Christ. This attitude of reverence for the achievements of the ancient philosophers Justin registers in the suggestion that the source of their wisdom was God himself. But his respect for philosophy is tempered by an acknowledgment that the tradition in which the teaching of the ancients has been handed down is full of errors and distortions; and these departures from truth require as much explanation as do the acceptable elements in the philosophical tradition. Therefore, Justin appeals to current schematizations of the history of philosophy which teach that an original deposit of truth has been deformed and dismembered by the successors of those who first received the revelation.

But Justin has a second, more memorable, and to him apparently more convincing means of accounting for the ambiguous status of Greek philosophy when it is brought before the bar of Scripture. This is the famous "loan" theory, which had been used already by Philo of Alexandria, from whom, directly or indirectly, Justin may well have derived it. This theory, like the former, is based on historical premises. Justin sets it forth in several passages. Thus, he argues in one place that Plato's doctrine of "creation," as formulated in the *Timaeus,* is borrowed from the account given in Genesis I:1–3.[14] Elsewhere, he explains himself in more general terms:

> Moses . . . is more ancient than all the Greek authors. And whatever philosophers and poets said about the immortality of the soul, or punishments after death, or contemplation of celestial phenomena, or other teachings of the same kind, they were able to understand and explain because they took up the suggestions of the prophets.[15]

This is, among other things, an interesting list of elements in the philosophical tradition which Justin is prepared to accept. He accepts them, however, not as merely consonant with the doctrine of the Scriptures, but as derived from them by a process of borrowing. They are, as a matter of fact, scriptural doctrines by origin; and this conclusion Justin establishes by calling attention to the chronological priority of Moses to the Greek philosophers.

The force of Justin's contention, for his readers as for himself, rests on three assumptions. The first, and for our purposes perhaps the most significant, is his conviction that in fact, as far as the doctrines which he specifies are concerned, the teaching of the philosophers and of the Hebrew Scriptures are more or less identical. This amounts to a tacit acknowledgment that the content of Christian belief is partially reproduced in Platonic theology. When Justin reads the words of Timaeus, he hears the accents of Moses, and vice versa.

The second assumption is the purely historical one of the superior antiquity of the Scriptures. Apparently, Justin is prepared to think that if two documents of different date contain many of the same ideas, the later of them must be dependent upon the earlier for its thought. He does not trouble himself to inquire whether there is any reason to believe that Plato had consulted the Hebrew Scriptures. Given the fact that Moses lived before Plato, Justin is prepared to believe that Moses' was the original version of the doctrines on which the two are agreed. But further—and this is Justin's third, equally silent, assumption—the antiquity of Moses would argue not merely that he is the source of Plato, but that his is the pure and definitive form of the teaching they share. The older wisdom is the more authentic and trustworthy.

The "loan" theory thus has as its essential point a critical judgment on the value of Greek theology. It asserts the primary and exclusive authority of the Scriptures as a source of guidance in the quest for God. To be sure, there is a great deal of truth in what the philosophers taught. But this truth is part and parcel of the revelation given to the prophets. Its authority is *their* authority, and it is to them that one must turn for the truth in its undistorted form. Moreover, Justin argues implicitly that the story of man's search for God is the history of the reception of that revelation which makes Christ known as its fulfillment. Plato learned the substance of his wisdom from the prophets. But the prophets announce Christ as the substance of their message. In the Christ, therefore, is to be sought the criterion and the completion of all "philosophy."

There is a close relation between this "loan" theory and the third, and most difficult, of Justin's theories about the status of Greek philosophy: his appeal to the idea of the *Logos spermatikos*. This conception, whose precise meaning has been the subject of not a little debate, is set forth in a number of passages, of which the following is one of the more explicit:

. . . each man [Justin is referring to the Greek poets and philosophers] spoke well according as he perceived, in proportion to his share in the seed-sowing divine Logos, its resemblance. But men who contradict themselves on points of central importance do not seem to have attained an understanding of hidden things and an unshakable knowledge. Hence whatever things have been truly said among all men belong to us Christians. For after God himself, we worship and love the Logos who comes to us from the ingenerate and ineffable God, since he also became man for our sakes. . . . For all the [Greek] authors were able to perceive Reality dimly on account of the indwelling sowing of the Logos which is implanted in them. For the seed and likeness of something, given according to the capacity of the recipient, is one thing; and quite another is the thing itself, in which men share and whose likeness they possess according to the grace which comes from him.[16]

The general meaning of this obscure passage is plain enough. Justin is saying that the Greek philosophers did indeed have an apprehension of the truth, but that their grasp of it was partial and limited. In Christ, however, whom Christians know as the Logos of God, the truth itself, whole and unsullied by error, is manifested to men.

But we can understand Justin more exactly if we look more

closely at his conception of the "Logos." In the Jewish Scriptures as rendered into Greek, "Logos" means the *Word* of God, that is, God active in creation, redemption, and self-revelation. But the term also had a specific meaning in the Greek philosophical tradition. Signifying both "reason" and "rational speech," "Logos" was one of the words which the Stoics had used to denote the cosmic Spirit by whose operation the world was held together, ordered, and governed. The human reason was in turn taken to be a "ray" or "fragment"—that is, a part— of this cosmic Logos. The Stoics further taught that as a result of universal and uniform human experience, man's *logos* or reason gives rise to certain "common conceptions," which the Stoics regarded as the "seeds" or principles of the basic religious and ethical beliefs which are shared by all men. Thus, the divine Logos, in the human reason, is *spermatikos*: it gives rise to the germinal notions or "seeds" of man's knowledge of God and of the principles of conduct.

Justin, then, in the passage which we have cited, is employing a Stoic idea to extend the meaning of the scriptural "Word of God." But he employs this Stoic idea in a non-Stoic form. His use of the conception of the Logos reflects the transformation of the original Stoic notion through its incorporation into a Platonist system. The character of this transformation can be observed in the writings of such authors as Philo and Plutarch. The Logos is identified with the Platonist World Soul, and is understood to be an immaterial Mind rather than a physical Energy. Further, in the Platonist scheme the human reason is no longer a "fragment" of the cosmic Reason, but rather an inferior substance which "participates" or "has a share in" the divine Reason. On a Platonist reading, therefore, the *Logos spermatikos* is the divine Reason which illuminates the human mind. And the "seeds" or the "sowing" of the Logos is the product of that illumination: a "sharing in" the Logos which is at the same time a discernment of the truth which is in God.

But "sharing in" is not possessing: and this is Justin's point in the passage we have been discussing. Human knowledge is only a part, a distant "resemblance," of the truth which is to be found in the divine Reason. Therefore, this knowledge cannot be weighed on the same scales as the original which it dimly imitates. On the other hand, it is not to be despised or depreciated. Even in its imperfection it represents a genuine trafficking with Reality. Thus, Justin can praise the philosophers for their perception of divine truth. But still he finds a great contrast between their case and that of the Christians, "who live not according to a [mere] share in the *Logos spermatikos,* but by knowledge and contemplation of the whole Logos, which is Christ." [17]

Now we are in a position to reconstruct Justin's teaching with some care. He takes it that the universal source of moral and religious knowledge for men is the illumination of the divine Logos, who is understood in two perspectives at once. He is both the active and powerful Word of the Scriptures, and the cosmic Mind of Middle Platonic philosophy. In this Logos all men "participate"; and it is the distinction of Greek philosophy that it has given such expression to the truth as can be attained on the basis of this universal participation of men in the divine Reason. But this Logos, who is the sole source of all man's knowledge of divine things, is also the one who in Christ has made himself wholly known to those who will believe. It follows then that in Christ incarnate is available the full and definitive form of that truth which the philosopher can know only in a limited way. Hence, Christ supersedes as he fulfills the truth which was available to men through the teachings of Socrates, Plato, and the Stoics.

In assessing this position, we are bound to see that Justin's identification of Christ as the divine Reason represents a crucial step in the assimilation of Christianity to the Hellenistic world. The earliest Christian apologetic had necessarily been dedicated to the task of showing that Christ was the fulfillment of the revelation of God given in the history of the Jewish people. But the history of Israel was important only to that small number of people who could regard it as in some sense their own. It was the apologetic merit of Justin's Logos doctrine that it explicitly claimed the history of Greek thought, the common cultural heritage of the Mediterranean world, as a part of the story of Christ's revelation of God. Christ as Logos becomes the universal mediator of the knowledge of God, and as such the culmination of the history not merely of Israel but of the entire "inhabited world." Thus, in principle Justin identifies "salvation history" with world history in a new way and to a new end when he insists that it was Christ and no other whom the philosophers dimly knew through their natural "participation" in the Logos.

But it requires to be emphasized that Justin's teaching is meant to insist upon the sufficiency of Christ. The idea of the *Logos spermatikos,* taken in its most straightforward sense, says no more than that Christ is that truth which naturally illumines the minds of all men and implants in them those rudimentary moral and religious conceptions which are the common stock of human piety. Justin is *not* saying that to read the philosophers is to know Christ. He is saying that to know Christ is to be able to dispense with philosophy. And if an adversary should retort that the teachings of the philosophers are by no means so rudimentary, dim, and platitudinous as Justin's theory would suggest; that the numerous pages of the *Timaeus* contain more than just reiterations of religious commonplaces; then Justin has answers to these as well. He can revert to his "loan" theory and argue that the cosmology of the *Timaeus* is borrowed in its essentials from Scripture. Justin wants, in one way or another, to deny the present necessity of a philosophical wisdom, even while he admits the partial validity of the insights of the Greek thinkers. The history of man's intellectual search for God is itself both a work of Christ and an anticipation of Christ. It is not a substitute for him. If, then, Justin is to teach doctrines which seem to have their roots in a secular intellectual tradition, it will always be upon the ground that they are in reality *scriptural* doctrines —a policy in which he has not a few modern followers.

GREEK IDEAS IN JUSTIN'S THEOLOGY

Nor can it be doubtful that as a matter of fact Justin did find, in Christian tradition and in the Jewish Scriptures, much that corresponded to the doctrines of the philosophers. We have already seen that he used the idea of the *Logos spermatikos* as an equivalent for, or an interpretation of, the Old Testament conception of the Word of God. He seems to have assumed without conscious question that these two notions, both rendered by the same Greek word, made reference to the same reality. Of course, his assumption was a perfectly natural one, which had highly respectable Jewish and Christian precedent; and it enabled him, as we have noted, to view the history of Greek thought on the analogy of the history of God's self-revelation in the Old Covenant, and thus to claim it as preparation for Christ.

But the Logos idea, in its Greek form, had a context, and therefore consequences, of its own. To envisage or interpret the Word of God as Logos was immediately to insert the biblical idea into the world-picture of a Greek theological cosmology. And this procedure, in turn, had two correlative results. It brought about a Hellenization of the scriptural conception, while at the same time it compelled a modification of the philosophical notions which were being used to elucidate the status of the Word of God. It is such a process of mutual adaptation which we shall be observing as we note how Justin uses themes drawn from the tradition of Greek thought to explain the meaning of certain central Christian teachings.

Let us first look more closely at his treatment of the Word, or Son, of God. It has already been pointed out that in Middle Platonic circles where the Stoic Logos idea was appropriated, the natural tendency was to identify the Logos with the World Soul of the *Timaeus* myth. It is therefore not surprising to find such a Platonist as Plutarch referring to the Mind which governs the world by the Stoic name of "Reason." What is perhaps more surprising is to discover that Justin, a Christian author, identifies the biblical "Son of God"—which for him, of course, simply means Christ—with the World Soul of the *Timaeus*.

The passage in question occurs in *I Apology* 60.1 ff. Justin is illustrating his view that Plato drew on the Scriptures for certain of his ideas. Having already instanced the notion of creation, he turns to another case: "Also there is the passage in Plato's *Timaeus* which discusses the Son of God. There Plato says, 'He placed him cross-wise in the universe.' " [18] The passage in the *Timaeus* which Justin cites (inaccurately) describes how the Craftsman set the World Soul within the Universe in such a way as to produce the most perfectly harmonious whole. But Justin also has in mind a biblical text, Numbers 21:7 f., which speaks of a brazen serpent which Moses set up on a "standard" in the wilderness—a serpent able to heal those who gazed upon it. This serpent with its healing powers had become for Christians a symbol of Christ lifted up on the Cross (John 3:14 f.) —a symbol, that is, both of the Cross itself and of the Son of God, who was there crucified. Hence, Justin argues, when Plato talks of the World Soul stretched out in the form of a cross (Plato means the Greek letter X), he can only be referring to the Son of God—and can only have got his original idea from reading Numbers!

We must not permit awe at the ingenuity of Justin's reasoning to distract attention from the central fact to which it bears witness. Justin thinks that when Plato talks about the World Soul, he is talking, though confusedly and at secondhand, about the Son of God, who is the Logos. Or, to put it another way, Justin sees in the World Soul, as the Platonism of his day understood it, an imperfect portrait of the Christ, or Word, which is begotten of God.

The plausibility of this identification does not in reality depend on Justin's farfetched argument about Plato's use of Scripture. Rather, it depends on the fact that in certain respects the character and functions of the Platonist World Soul correspond to those of the Word, or Wisdom, of God as conceived in late Judaism and early Christianity. For one thing, just as the Word is (for Justin) a divine being "numerically distinct" [19] from God the Father; so the World Soul is a divine Mind distinct from the supreme Intelligence that Middle Platonists acknowledged as the First God.

But there is more to Justin's identification than this. The Scriptures were clear in their teaching that God's creation of the world was by his Word; and Christians, employing an idea which was widespread in Judaism, had not hesitated to assign to Christ, the Word who became incarnate, a role in the cosmos as the instrumental cause of creation and the one "in whom all things consist." [20] But the Platonist World Soul was also conceived to play a cosmic mediatorial role—and one not obviously unlike that assigned by Christians to the Word. Albinus, for example, writes that the First God "aroused the Soul of the World and turned it to himself, being the source of its intelligence—that intelligence which, when put in order by the Father, puts into order the whole of nature in this world." [21] In this view, the First God works indirectly in fashioning the world, and the immediate job of ordering the cosmos is assigned to the World Soul. But does not this conception reflect the biblical picture? Is it not true that for the Bible God always deals with the world *through his Word?* Is it not by his Word that God is present in the world to create, to reveal himself, and to redeem? What more reasonable, then, than to see in the Platonist World Soul an image of Christ?

Of course, the correspondence is not exact. The Platonist doctrine fails, among other things, to explain that the Logos is indeed the *Son* of God: not merely a Mind eternally coexisting with God but deity born of deity, generated or begotten of the Father to work his will in creation and redemption. In this respect, at any rate, the philosophical conception of the World Soul had to be revised to meet the requirements of Christian faith. But as a scheme for understanding the role of Christ in the world and the way in which God relates himself to the cosmic order—for these purposes, it seemed to serve admirably. What, then, did it imply about the nature of God and his relation to the universe, and how far were its implications appropriated in Justin's teaching? Let us look.

JUSTIN AND THE UNIQUENESS OF GOD

If the Son of God is the World Soul/Logos, what about the Father? In a Stoic system, there could be no answer to this Christian question, because the Stoics knew no divine power above the cosmic Reason. But the question could find an answer of sorts from a Middle Platonist point of view, since, as we have noticed, the Middle Platonists tended to turn Plato's mythical Craftsman into a Mind transcendent over the world. They even referred to him, following Plato's language,[22] as the Father and Maker of the world. It was quite logical, therefore, for Justin, who saw in the World Soul a version of the Son of God, to find in the Craftsman a type of God himself. That this is in fact so is indicated by the presence of some eight passages (all in the apologies, which are addressed to pagan audiences) in which the word "Craftsman" or its related verb, meaning "to fashion," is used to refer to the Christian God. Thus, in one place where he carefully distinguishes between the Word and God himself, Justin describes the latter as "the Father and Craftsman of the universe."[23] Similarly, he accuses the heretic Marcion of teaching that there is another God besides "the Craftsman of all,"[24] and protests that Christians are not atheists, but worshipers of "the Craftsman of this universe."[25]

The reasons why Justin adopts this way of speaking should be fairly obvious. The First God of Middle Platonic philosophy was conceived in a way which seemed in many respects to correspond with the scriptural characterization of God. Although he could not be thought of as a subject of action bearing upon the world, he was, nevertheless, as the final source of Being, the Author of the world. Moreover, he was clearly and emphatically set apart from the world. Philosophers applied to him a series of epithets which were intended to assert his transcendence over the universe—a transcendence which was conceived not spatially but ontologically. When a writer like Albinus spoke of the First God as ingenerate, incomprehensible, indivisible, and immortal, he was attempting to spell out the difference between the universe with all its members and that Reality which is no part or aspect or quality of the cosmic order because it is its Source and Ground.

To Justin, nothing seemed more natural than to adopt language of this sort to express the majesty and uniqueness of the Christian God. Following the Middle Platonists and Philo, he describes God habitually as "ingenerate" and "ineffable." He speaks of him also as "impassible" and "nameless." Such descriptions serve, for him, the obvious purpose of asserting the supremacy and ultimacy of the God that the Scriptures call "the Lord." God has no name because there is none before him to name him; and he is ingenerate because, being immortal and incorporeal, he has no source of his being.

At the same time, these terms and others like them inevitably assume, for Justin, the function of defining the distinction between God and the world, and thus the manner of his transcendence over it. The God of Jewish and Christian faith, trusted, loved, and feared as the Ruler of world history, was no comprehensible force with whom men could deal as a familiar and unvarying factor in the cosmic equation. He was outside human control and calculation, eternally strange and majestically holy even in his nearness and his mercy. His glory admitted of no comparison between himself and his creatures. This biblical sense of God's "beyondness" Justin tries to capture by use of the same language which he employs to affirm the ultimacy of God. Words like "ingenerate" and "impassible" set God over against the world by making implicit use of the Platonic distinction between Being—or the Source of Being—and Becoming. God is the apex of the eternal and changeless order of intelligible reality; and as such he is "beyond" the mutable and perishable world which is his creation.

Justin does not, however, perceive that his appropriation of the negative language of Middle Platonist theology conceals an ambiguity and a problem. "Being" and "Becoming"—or "ingenerate" and "generate"—denote, in a Platonist system, logical contraries. That is, speaking loosely, they stand for opposed qualities within a single "spectrum." Consequently, the realities which they name *exclude each other;* and God's transcendence over the world, when figured in terms of the contrast between Being and Becoming, turns out to be a form of necessary separation from the world. He is, ontologically speaking, outside the world and can enter into relation with it only through a mediating agency —that of the cosmic Reason, or Logos. There were in Platonist thought resources which might possibly have enabled Justin to escape this definition of divine transcendence in terms of a logical opposition between ingenerate and generate existence. He might have asked, for example, what were the implications of the statement that God is "beyond Being." [26] This expression could be taken as suggesting that God is "beyond" relations either of identity with, or of opposition to, members of the visible world-order, because he cannot be thought of as belonging to the same logical "spectrum" as they. But the evidence indicates that Justin did not see this possible meaning of the language that he employed, or, rather, that he did not grasp the problem in the first place. He continued to define God's transcendence in a way which made his "glory" inconsistent with his active presence within the world.

There was, however, one problem associated with the adoption of this terminology which Justin did not fail to perceive or to deal with. Having used the language of Platonist theology to explain the ultimacy and the transcendence of God, he saw, if only half-consciously, that of itself it did not satisfy the demand of Christian faith for a God one and unique. This sensitivity to the issue between monotheism and polytheism was, of course, a necessary part of the equipment of a Christian apologist in the second century; and Justin took care to make it plain that for him the term "ingenerate" was not the name of a class of many possible beings, but the name of a class with only one member: God. This entailed, whether Justin realized it or not, a drastic revision of the Platonist world-picture, which had described (among other things) all intelligences as ingenerate and divine. But, for Justin, there could be only one God. The Father/Craftsman was, for him, the "sole ingenerate,"[27] the unique and ultimate Reality who was the object of man's religious search.

THE WORLD AS CREATED

But if he says that God is the "sole ingenerate," what is thereby implied about the world and its status? The obvious answer to this question is that the world must be conceived as "generate," that is, as "Becoming" rather than "Being." This reply, however, is incomplete until we know what Justin took the word "generate" to connote in this connection. For Middle Platonism it ordinarily meant just one thing: that the material world-order is by nature an eternal process of change and decay, which can therefore only imperfectly realize the rational stability of Being. But it was not taken to imply that the world had a "beginning."

This view, though, had already been attacked by the Jewish philosopher Philo, himself a disciple of the new Platonism. "There are some people," he writes,

who, having the world in admiration rather than the Maker of the world, pronounce it to be without beginning and everlasting, while with impious falsehood they postulate in God a vast inactivity . . .[28]

Philo then goes on to argue that there are two reasons why it is necessary to assign a temporal beginning to the world. The first is that to deny the world a beginning is to deny the beneficence and providential care of God, and thus to regard the world-order as an anarchic "disorder." The second is that the word "generate" implies origination in whatever it is applied to. For whatever is visible, changeable, and corruptible must have a beginning as surely as it will have an end. Philo thus criticizes his Platonist contemporaries—with what logical force it is not for us to inquire —in order to assert the biblical teachings that God is active in his relation to the world and that the world has its origin in his creative activity.

Justin agrees with Philo. Confronted with the same set of problems, he thinks that there are two fundamental adjustments which must be made in normal Platonist teaching if it is to be brought into accord with its revealed scriptural original. One of these we have already alluded to: it is implicit in Justin's assertion that the Father is "sole ingenerate." Whatever is not God is made by him and therefore "generate"; and this class notably includes the human soul, which, even if God wills it not to pass out of existence, must nevertheless be regarded as having an existence which is derived and not independent. But further, Justin is sure that the Christian must agree with Moses and Plato against the "so-called Platonists" [29] in denying the eternity of the world. In his view, the world is generate not only in the sense of being visible and corruptible but also in the sense of having a beginning. As a Platonist, he proposes to take the myth of the *Timaeus* literally; and as a Christian he sees in this myth the rough equivalent—indeed, the derivative—of the creation story in Genesis. Christians, he tells the Emperor Antoninus, "have been taught that [God] at the beginning, because he is good, did fashion all things out of unformed matter";[30] and "Plato borrowed his opinion that God made a world-order" [31]— borrowed it, to be specific, from Moses, who explains in Genesis "how and out of what materials God fashioned the world-order." [32] Thus are creatures "made," "generated," "founded and ordered," according to Justin. The world is not eternal. It has a

beginning in the creative activity of God, who out of chaos produces order, through the mediating agency of his Logos.

It might reasonably be asked, on the basis of this evidence,
whether Justin looked any more deeply into the problem of creation than he did into that of divine transcendence. Consistently
with his treatment of the ideas of God and the Son of God, he
views the world as the realm of "Becoming," the *generate* order.
But his development of this idea is doubly puzzling. To the
Platonist, for example, his inclusion of soul in the category of
that which has "come to be" was bound to seem the product of
mere lack of understanding. What sense could it make to envisage knowledge of God as the destiny of a life intrinsically
bound up with change and corruption? On the other hand, the
Jew or Christian might plausibly wonder whether Justin's idea
of the world's "beginning" was not defective. He assigns to God
the initiation of the world *as a rationally ordered whole,* reading
Genesis in the light of Plato's myth of creation. But does this
doctrine represent an adequate rendering of the biblical sense
of God's absolute and unqualified initiative with reference to the
world? When a Christian speaks of the "beginning" of the
world, is he referring merely to God's bringing order out of
chaos, or does he mean to assert God's responsibility for the very
existence of anything apart from himself? Justin, in fact, does
not seem to have posed this question to himself at all. At any
rate, he supplies no clear answer to it.

But we will return again to the question of the problems
which Justin left behind him. For the moment, we must take
time to reflect on the way in which his practical use of Platonist
themes in his theology corresponds to his view of the relation
between Greek philosophy and Christian teaching. It should be
clear that, in his own mind, Justin is expounding the doctrine
which he finds in the Jewish Scriptures as the meaning of these
is made plain in Christ and in the preaching of the Apostolic
Church. He uses philosophical ideas, not systematically or spec-
ulatively, but pragmatically. That is, he employs them as and

when they seem to him to coincide with the teaching of the Scriptures. Where, on the other hand, they appear to him to deviate from this teaching, he either revises them to fit his model or ignores them. Furthermore, it is just this policy which accounts for the puzzles in Justin's thought: the inconsistencies and superficialities which dog the steps of his expositions. Neither his use nor his revision of philosophical ideas is governed by the scientific impulse to present a coherent view of the world. Rather, it is motivated by his wish to clarify and interpret certain major themes in Christian teaching by fitting them into a readjusted Platonist world-picture. In consequence, his apologetic has a tentative, and even haphazard, quality about it when it is viewed from the perspective of rational theology. The tendencies of his thought are clear; his precise position on a given question is not always clear. And this difficulty is only aggravated by the fact that Justin is not a philosophical thinker of any great depth, learning, or dialectical skill.

PROBLEMS FOR THE FUTURE

If we ask, therefore, what it is that Justin hands on to his successors, we have to conclude that it is a set of problems which are bound up with the central themes of his philosophical apologetic. Justin himself, of course, is more than an apologist; and his apologetic, with certain aspects of which we have dealt here, by no means represents the heart or the sum of his Christian faith. It does, however, represent his distinctive contribution to the continuing stream of Christian thought; and this, not because it was taken over uncritically, but because it helped to create and to define the *issues* of later theology. We must now indicate what some of these issues were.

The root of the principal problems generated by Justin's theology seems to be a single one. It is found in the basic idea which governs the Middle Platonic world-picture: the distinction between the orders of Being and Becoming, ingenerate and generate existence, which Justin employs and adapts to define the difference between God and world. In its Platonist form, as we have seen, this distinction served many purposes and had many implications. It provided the theoretical framework within which philosophers elaborated their view of the world as a static hierarchical order—an order created and sustained by that knowledge of Being which enables soul, or mind, at once to realize its kinship with the Divine and at the same time to "rationalize" the chaotic motions of matter. Understood in the light of man's religious quest, this conception supplied both an answer to the problem of evil and an account of human nature and destiny. Man, it explained, is essentially soul, an eternal principle of intelligent life. His trouble and affliction derives from his involvement in the irrationalities of material existence; and his proper end is to realize through knowledge and the practice of virtue his kinship with intelligible Reality.

Some of the problems created by Justin's use, and his revisions, of this scheme have already been indicated. His account of creation, for example, reflects a critical adaptation of Platonist ideas. He insists, in effect, upon revising both the connotation and the denotation of the expression "generate existence." Thus, the word "generate" no longer suggests merely the sort of being which is material and unstable. It also means "dependent for existence upon the initiative of God," and therefore, as applied to the world and its members, entails the belief that they have (or had) a "beginning." Moreover, it now encompasses in its denotation everything which is not God. We have already noticed Justin's insistence that soul cannot, in a Christian scheme, be regarded as eternal. This does not mean that he wants to surrender the Platonist conception of the soul's nature and destiny as *mind*. He still holds, though in a new sense, to the ideas that soul is deathless and that "contemplation of things divine" [33] is its destiny. Even so, however, it must (somewhat paradoxically from a Platonist viewpoint) be classed as "generate," since God must be acknowledged as the source of its existence and at the same time as "sole ingenerate."

But these revisions themselves leave unsettled problems behind them. Justin, for example, seems uncertain whether matter as well as soul has its source in the creative power of God. Does matter then represent an independent principle, a limitation on the initiative of God, as it does for the Platonist Craftsman? If so, Justin would appear to call in question his Christian belief in the absoluteness of God's power. Or is it that Justin feels—unconsciously perhaps—that the irrationality of matter must be appealed to for an explanation of disorder and evil in the world, as it is on a Platonist view? If so, what becomes of the biblical sense of the goodness of the material order and its capacity for redemption? Or for that matter, what happens to the scriptural conviction that disorder and evil in the world are due ultimately to *sin:* that is, not to the influence of external conditions on the soul, but to the rebellion of the creature against its creator? There is no indication that Justin was aware that his theological procedures raised these questions; but they represent problems implicit in his position.

Again, what of Justin's identification of God with ingenerate Being *as opposed to Becoming?* Being, in a Platonist system, represents a static Object of contemplation and desire. Set apart from the visible order, it influences the world because it is the vision which fills the mind and directs the activity of soul. Almost thoughtlessly, Justin dresses this Deity in the attributes of the scriptural God, the God who takes steps, who is active in creation and redemption. But how can a Deity whose nature is alien to change and becoming be the creative initiator of change, involved and active in the world he makes? Justin's doctrine of divine transcendence raises this question in a vivid form.

Of course, he offers an answer. The ingenerate and immutable Father realizes his purposes (but in what sense does the Platonist Deity have "purposes"?) through the mediatorial activity of the Logos. This answer, however, creates as many problems as it solves. For one thing, it seems merely to emphasize the exclusion of God from the world. For another, it poses the thorny problem of the status of the Logos. Is he generate or ingenerate? Is he God (and if so, are there *two* Gods?) or is he a creature? Justin replies that he is generate—but in a special sense. He is God born of God, as fire is kindled by fire, or light is produced from the sun.[34] That is, he is divine, but in a derivative or secondary way. Here, Justin's Christian faith and the logic of his revised Platonist world-picture drag him in opposite directions. He wants the Logos to be the same sort of thing as the Father (the *Son* of God), and at the same time to be a distinct and slightly inferior sort of Deity, like the Platonist World Soul. In short, he wants to associate the Logos both with Being and with Becoming, both with God and world. Consequently, he must describe him as "God generate"—an expression which, in different ways, seems to violate both Greek and Christian conceptions of God, and leaves the status of the Logos and the meaning of his "generation" in some doubt.

Finally, there is implicit in Justin's use of philosophical ideas a problem about the nature of man and of man's redemption. Here, the word "implicit" is the important one; for Justin almost never addresses himself directly to questions of this order. Nevertheless, the Platonist world-picture which Justin adapted involved both a conception of what man is and an ideal of the blessed human life; and Justin inevitably incorporated these into his understanding of Christianity, setting them alongside biblical ideas with which they did not always cohere. Thus, there can be little doubt that he tends to think of man as a rational soul whose natural destiny is the immortal life which flows from likeness to God and the knowledge of God. On the other hand, he not only insists upon the Christian-Jewish dogma of a resurrection of the body—a notion almost incomprehensible by Platonist lights; but he also emphasizes, with an appreciation of the meaning of what he says, that the soul itself is "generate," and therefore not *of itself* immortal. He makes no attempt to reconcile these contrary sets of ideas or to explain how it is possible to make sense of a quasi-Platonist ideal of redemption while denying its normal presuppositions. But the problem remains implicit in his thought; and future Christian thinkers will have to deal with it more explicitly.

It may be that if we had more of Justin's writing, we should find that he had offered further reflections on some of these problems. As it is, however, we can only note them as a product of his attempt to reconcile Christian teaching with a Platonist world-picture, and then try to see how certain of his successors dealt with them.

Notes to Chapter II

1. *I Apology*, Preface.
2. *Ecclesiastical History* IV.11.11.
3. *Ibid.* IV.11.8.
4. *Martyrdom of St. Justin* 2.
5. H.-Ch. Puech, *Histoire de la littérature Grecque Chrétienne* II.133 f.
6. *Dialogue with Trypho* 2.1–8.2.
7. *Ibid.* 1.3 *ad fin.*, and 2.1.
8. *Ibid.* 2.1.
9. *Ibid.* 2.6.
10. *Ibid.* 4.1.
11. *Ibid.* 7.3.
12. *Ibid.* 8.1 f.
13. *Ibid.* 3.4.
14. *I Apology* 59.1–5.
15. *Ibid.* 44.8–9.
16. *II Apology* 13.3–6.
17. *Ibid.* 8.3.
18. For the quotation from Plato, see *Timaeus* 36 B.
19. *Dialogue with Trypho* 56.11.
20. *Colossians* 1.17.
21. *Epitome* X.3.
22. Cf. *Timaeus* 28 C.
23. *I Apology* 63.11.
24. *Ibid.* 58.1.
25. *Ibid.* 13.1.
26. See pp. 25 ff., 34 f.
27. *Dialogue with Trypho* 5.4.
28. *De opificio mundi* 7 (tr. Colson and Whitaker).
29. *Dialogue with Trypho* 5.1.
30. *I Apology* 10.2.
31. *Ibid.* 59.1.
32. *Ibid.*
33. *Ibid.* 58.3.
34. *Dialogue with Trypho* 128.

CHAPTER III. *Irenaeus and the Gnostic Problem*

AMONG THE heirs of Justin's apologetic was a much younger contemporary, Irenaeus, Bishop of Lyons, in southern Gaul, around A.D. 180. Irenaeus, however, was by no means a mere disciple or follower of Justin's. He did in fact respect and draw upon the teaching of the Roman martyr. But Justin's writings were only one among many sources which Irenaeus tapped in the pursuit of his own theological interests. These interests, moreover, were themselves of a rather different order from those which had shaped Justin's apologies. The Gaulish Bishop was struggling not against pagan misunderstanding of Christianity, but against a sectarian movement within the Church itself. His principal work, the *Adversus Haereses,** was directed against the teaching of a group of so-called Gnostics, and it exhibits the cautious mentality and essentially conservative intent which one might expect in a treatise meant to refute what its author regards as dangerous doctrinal innovation. But Irenaeus differs from Justin in yet another crucial respect. He was most emphatically not a philosopher turned Christian. Indeed, he was not a convert at all, but a child of the Church. His theology, in consequence, is a weaving together of patterns of

* The full and proper title of this work is *A Scrutiny and Refutation of the Falsely Named 'Knowledge'*; but the shorter title has been universally adopted for convenience.

71

thought which he, as a Christian from birth, held to be authentic elements in the tradition handed on from Christ's Apostles. Called the father of Christian orthodoxy, and not without reason, Irenaeus was thus not only the heir but also, implicitly, the critic of Justin's ideas; and to him we may look for a reconsideration, in the light of new problems, of the central ideas of Justin's theology.

But before it is possible to discuss this development directly, we must take the time to understand more, in a general way, of Irenaeus's background, his outlook and equipment as a Christian thinker, and the issues which he was called upon by the circumstances of his time to face. No more than other Christian authors of his era does Irenaeus write out of an interest in the problems of theology for their own sake. His work is, in the strictest sense, occasional, motivated by pastoral rather than purely intellectual concerns. In consequence, what he has to say and the way in which he says it are jointly determined by the concrete situation to which he addressed himself.

THE PHENOMENON OF GNOSIS

Despite the fact that he is remembered as the bishop of a church in southern Gaul, Irenaeus was not a native of Gaul or of any western part of the Roman Empire. He came from Asia Minor, and his native tongue was Greek. He may well have been born in Smyrna, for he reports that as a child he had seen the sainted Polycarp, who had been bishop in that city. In any case, it was Christianity as he had learned it in the place of his birth and education which he regarded as normative for the Church's belief. This faith, fed by memories of the holy men who had taught it, Irenaeus brought with him to the West. There he found it upheld and confirmed by the traditions of the one Western Church which would boast of apostolic foundation. This was, of course, the Roman Church, which was itself Greek-speaking at this time, and numbered a substantial group of believers from Asia Minor among its members.

At Lyons, where he served first as a presbyter, and where he became bishop after the martyrdom of his predecessor, Pothinus, Irenaeus found that this form of belief was being questioned and corrupted. Christians there, and not there alone, as he knew, were being seduced from the original form of their faith in Christ. They were being led astray by men who claimed to possess a deeper truth, of which the ordinary teachings of the Church were only symbols and distant intimations. The content of this deeper truth, which its adherents called *gnosis,* or "knowledge," concerned the fundamental religious question of the origin, nature, and destiny of the soul. It was an esoteric doctrine, this: by no means intended for every man, since, it was taught, not every man had the natural capacity to receive it. But those who were able to receive it—the *gnostikoi,* those "in the know" —constituted a religious elite who could believe that they had grasped the genuine essence of revelation and that their salvation was thereby assured. It is no wonder that Irenaeus had to complain that these men were overthrowing the faith of many, or that he was forced to acknowledge the seductiveness of their teaching. Gnosticism gave the appearance of being Christian. It took, or could take, the form of an interpretation of the Church's Scriptures, and was therefore well calculated to engage the interest of the faithful. At the same time, it appealed not only to men's self-esteem and their desire for security and certainty but also to deep and quite honest religious impulses. The trouble was, in Irenaeus's view, that Gnosis was not so much a version as it was a simple contradiction of Christianity, a denial of its central teachings.

In cool retrospect, the historian can agree with much in Irenaeus's estimate of Gnosticism. The Bishop of Lyons was well aware that the movement he was opposing was not of recent or local origin. He followed other Christian writers—for example, Justin Martyr—in tracing its rise from the activities of

Simon the Magician, who is mentioned in the Book of Acts.[1] But, although Irenaeus admitted that a form of Gnosticism was at least as old as Christianity itself, and that the Gnostic movement had been the constant companion of the Church in its growth and spread, he was equally convinced that the springs of Gnosticism lay outside the sources of authentic Christian tradition.

As a matter of fact, this analysis of the historical situation, although imprecise, has more than a grain of truth in it. The question of the origins of Gnosticism is still a matter for debate. But it is now generally agreed that the movement, in its relation to Christianity, was not so much an interior product of the Church's life as a product of the marginal interaction of Christian beliefs with a particular current in Roman-Hellenistic religious thought. The sources of this current were manifold. Magical, astrological, and apocalyptic ideas were blended together with themes drawn from the mystery religions and the Greek philosophical tradition to make a truly strange and constantly varying mixture of occult teachings. It seems quite possible, however, that the cohesion and direction of this current are to be explained by its origins in circles associated with heterodox Judaism. In this view, Gnosticism grew up initially in places where ideas or symbols drawn from Jewish writings served as focuses for the creation of a synthetic religious doctrine. Such a hypothesis helps to explain not merely the origins of Gnosticism but also the fact that it had from the beginning so natural an affinity for Christianity, itself a child of Judaism. It also partly accounts for a writer like Irenaeus feeling that, despite the long history of "Christian" Gnosticism, the Gnostic movement was not a direct outgrowth, however unhealthy or perverted, of Christian life and thought, but rather a kind of penumbral Christianity, a doctrine whose alien substance was clothed in a shadow cast by the Gospel.

Part of the difficulty about understanding the origins and

character of Gnosticism derives from the fact that the movement took many forms and spawned numerous sects. Irenaeus himself, in the first book of the *Adversus Haereses,* where he gives an account of his adversaries' teaching, distinguishes better than a dozen "schools" within the movement; and although his statements are certainly not in all respects reliable, the impression which he deliberately conveys of the Protean nature of Gnosticism is undoubtedly a fair one. Gnosticism was not an organized movement, but a tendency of thought which could and did crystallize in many forms. It encompassed almost every kind of esoteric religion, from the practice of magic to the profound speculative explorations of Valentinus, the Alexandrian Gnostic who taught in Rome during the lifetime of Justin and Irenaeus.

Irenaeus himself, however, was not interested in Gnosis as a general phenomenon. His survey of the various Gnostic schools was meant simply to lay a foundation for his refutation of a particular form of teaching which he had personally met in Lyons and its environs, and with whose content he had had some direct acquaintance. This was the doctrine of one Ptolemy, "whose school," Irenaeus writes, "may be described as a bud from that of Valentinus." [2] Ptolemaean Gnosticism was thus a development or modification of the speculative system of Valentinus. As such, it was a system of phantasmagoric complexity, whose purpose was to depict the truth about the identity of the Gnostic in his innermost nature. This truth it conveyed in quasi-philosophical, quasi-mythological form, as it explained the origin of the world, of evil, and of the "spirit" that is the peculiar element in the constitution of the Gnostic. Irenaeus lays out the details of this system before proceeding to refute it; and we must follow him in an attempt to ascertain not so much what Gnosticism looked like to a Gnostic but what it looked like to its opponents.

A GNOSTIC SYSTEM

The essential note of the Ptolemaean Gnosis, as Irenaeus presents it, is a thoroughgoing dualism. The Gnostic acknowledged not one world, but two. The first—the original and noblest world—was the immortal realm of what he called "the Pleroma"—"the Fullness." This was a society of Divine Beings, or "Eons," at whose apex stood the unknown and unknowable Ultimate—"the Abyss." It was this divine world of which "spirit" was held to be a displaced native.

Outside and beneath the Pleroma was the material world, which was regarded as including within itself the very principle of evil. Between these two realms, the spiritual and the material, there was a connection, but a connection only indirect and tenuous. As the Gnostics saw it, the existence of the material world was the unintended product of a temporary disorder within the life of the Pleroma. They taught that one of the Divine Beings, or Eons, had been seized by an irrational desire to rise above itself to a knowledge of the incomprehensible God. Order could only be restored to the divine realm, and the sinning Eon be saved, by a purging of the Lust which had led it astray. Once this was done, tranquillity was renewed within the Pleroma— but only at the cost of leaving outside the Pleroma that same irrational Lust which "was nevertheless a spiritual being, possessing some of the natural impulses of an Eon, yet shapeless and formless on account of its lack of understanding." [3] The Ptolemaean Gnostics named this Lust "Achamoth," and in her they saw the principle of the material world.

The process, however, by which Achamoth produced the world was a complex one which reflected the complexity of her nature. According to the form of the Gnostic myth which Irenaeus relates, Achamoth was composed of three differing tendencies or capacities, each of which corresponded to an element in the constitution of the world which was generated out of her.

She was first of all a creature of passion in whom ignorance and frustrated desire had brought forth storms of disordered feeling; and this passion was the stuff of corporeal matter, irrational and formless. But she was also endowed with a sincere, though blind and ultimately fruitless, longing for the purity and truth of the Pleroma, from which she had been cast out; and this aspiration is the stuff of which soul is made—soul as it is found in men, in angels, and in the Demiurge: the Craftsman of the visible world. But finally, Achamoth was a "spiritual" nature, by reason of the fact that her substance was derived from the Pleroma itself. And the offspring of this spiritual nature, blended with certain souls without the knowledge of the Demiurge, are the "spirits" of the *gnostikoi*, destined ultimately, like Achamoth herself, to return to their home in the Pleroma.

In their present exile, however, these spirits live under the domination of an angelic deity, the Demiurge, who, since he is mere soul, is ignorant of any life higher than his own. It is his doings, we are told, and his purposes which are reflected in the history and sacred literature of the Jews. By the same token, the human and earthly Jesus is his Messiah. But the Gnostics taught that in the teaching of Jesus there is a hidden dimension of truth which makes known the higher reality of the Pleroma itself. For, they explained, a divine Eon, the Saviour, descended upon Jesus at his baptism and accompanied him till the moment of his suffering and death. Hence, the man who reads the words of Christ with an apprehension attuned to their inner meaning rather than to their literal significance finds in them not the words of the Jewish Messiah, the Promised One of the angelic Demiurge, but the teaching of the Saviour himself, which teaching conveys a knowledge of the divine life of the Pleroma.

It is a fantastic account, this. But its significance should not be forgotten in astonishment at the extravagance of its form. In all its mythological exuberance, this story eloquently portrays a drama of redemption in which the conflicts of man's inner life are objectified and projected on a cosmic screen. The symbolism of the myth is in large part psychological, and the truth which it conveys is a truth about the diverging tendencies or impulses which govern the life of man within the world-order. These impulses are interpreted by being shown to correspond to different levels of existence in external reality; and the fate of man is written out for all to read in the story of Achamoth. What Gnosticism offers is thus, in the first instance, a form of self-knowledge, spelled out in the shape of a cosmic drama of fall, creation, and redemption; and in this self-knowledge, salvation is found.

But the myth is also meant quite seriously as suggesting a world-picture commensurable with that offered by the rational theology of late Platonism—on which, in fact, it seems to be partly dependent. The radical dualism which Irenaeus notes and repudiates in the Ptolemaean system is in the first instance the expression of a religious attitude. But its plausibility in its time owed not a little to the fact that it was reminiscent of the dualism of Being and Becoming, which lay at the foundation of the Platonist cosmology. Furthermore, the Gnostic evaluation of matter was not without precedent or parallel in later Platonist speculation.

CONSEQUENCES OF GNOSTICISM

Nevertheless, the differences between these two views of the world and its structure are as basic as their similarities. The Gnostic tended to think of matter as a positive principle of evil and error. He could conceive of no natural relation between matter and spirit save that of complete mutual exclusion. Consequently, his world was not a continuous whole unfolding in a variety of forms between the two poles of material and intelligible existence. Rather, it consisted of distinct and contrary substances which should, ideally, be totally segregated from each other. The facts that matter exists and that matter, soul, and spirit are somehow "mixed" in the visible world-order are carefully explained as the result of two cosmic faux pas: that temporary disorder within the Pleroma which produced Achamoth, and the passion of Achamoth herself. Thus, morally as well as metaphysically, the Pleroma is separated from the visible world. The Gnostics even took the trouble to insist that the work of the angelic Creator who ordered the world was carried out in ignorance and independence of higher truth. Hence, such a writer as Irenaeus could claim with some justification that the Gnostics taught a doctrine of two Gods, denying both the goodness of the Creator and the omnipotence of the Father of the Pleroma. In their eagerness to segregate matter from spirit, evil from good, the Gnostics dissolved at once the unity of the world and the unity of God.

And in doing so, of course, they contradicted the spirit as well as the letter of the classical Platonic cosmology. This represented, after all, an attempt to portray the visible world as a providential order, reflecting in its constitution and its motions the rationality of the intelligible world. The myth of creation in the *Timaeus* had as one of its fundamental purposes to assert the unification and reconciliation of the material and spiritual orders through the agency of soul. And just as Platonism in its classical form thus insisted upon the unity and (relative) goodness of the visible world, so it tended, as we have seen, to seek one ultimate divine Principle which is the source of order and of being in both the visible and the invisible realms. The vestiges of this idea are present in Gnosticism; but it is transformed almost beyond recognition by the Gnostic conviction that matter and spirit are irreconcilable.

To Irenaeus, however, the Gnostic dissolution of the unity of the world-order was not half so important as its corresponding dissolution of the unity of salvation history: that is, of the history of God's dealings with man set forth in the sacred writings of the Church. The Gnostics dismissed the Old Testament and the revelation which it contained as largely inconsistent with the new truth which the Saviour had made known through Jesus.

In their view, the inspiration of Moses and the prophets was derived not from the ultimate God of the Pleroma, but from the angelic Creator-God who in his ignorance had proclaimed himself the sole Lord of heaven and earth. Traditional Christian exegesis had, of course, assumed that the God who made the world and then revealed himself to the Jews was the same God whose salvation is offered to mankind in Christ. Hence, it tended to envisage human history as a continuous whole which exhibited God's progressive realization of his purpose for men. But the Gnostics would have none of this. They interpreted the relation between Old Covenant and New, between Moses and Christ, in terms of their own dualism, and in this way set the one firmly in opposition to the other. The God of Moses for them was *not* the Father of Christ, any more than the redemption which they preached was a fulfillment of the Creator's purpose in making the world. The "knowledge" which they found hidden in the teaching of Jesus led them to a repudiation of all the work of the Creator—of the visible world which he had ordered, and of the revelation which he had given to the Jews. From their point of view, these gifts were the product of error; and the truth about man was only to be grasped by repudiating them. In this way, the Gnostic dualism destroyed the integrity of the theology of history which lay at the heart of Christian preaching.

Confronted with this system, Irenaeus undertook the laborious task of demonstrating its essential falsity. This enterprise, however, involved him in several distinct kinds of argument, which must be distinguished here, not only for the sake of noting the different dimensions of Irenaeus's thought, but also for the sake of understanding more of the background and sources of his teaching.

THE FORM OF IRENAEUS'S ARGUMENT

At one level, Irenaeus attacks the Gnostic system, or systems, by calling attention to what he regards as their logical absurdity. This form of argument is characteristic in particular of the second book of the *Adversus Haereses,* and its special object is the Gnostic idea of God. By a diligent use of the quasi-logical, quasi-rhetorical device of the dilemma, Irenaeus tries with some success to expose the inconsistencies of a view which proclaims the infinity and supremacy of the ultimate God while at the same time denying his responsibility for the material world. The rational and abstract character of this argument—whose persuasive force is enhanced by a tone of irony and ridicule which informs it—lends to it a speculative appearance which suggests that Irenaeus may be drawing to some extent on the resources of contemporary philosophical ideas. In fact, however, this appearance is largely, though not wholly, deceptive. The conceptions of Deity with which Irenaeus works undoubtedly have roots or associations in the philosophy of his time. Nevertheless, his mode of argumentation is highly personal. And what is more important, there is clear evidence in the second book of the *Adversus Haereses* itself that Irenaeus was prone to distrust philosophical speculation on the two grounds that it led to no certain or reliable conclusions, and that it was in any case the source of Gnosticism.

Irenaeus's hostility toward philosophy is quite explicit. From time to time, it is true, he uses expressions or makes statements which reflect Justin's rather "liberal" estimate of the status of Greek philosophy. He is not above quoting with approval some of Plato's views on God, drawn from the *Laws* and, of course, the *Timaeus.*[4] But his personal views are manifested more clearly when he labels philosophers generally as "ignorant of God,"[5] and describes their teachings as "a heap of miserable rags."[6] He makes use of a sort of pocket digest of the opinions of the philosophers and principal schools of philosophers; but only in order to draw out, somewhat ineptly, the parallels between these doctrines and those of the Gnostics. He points with obvious pleasure to the disagreements of the philosophers, who propound, he says, "many kinds of truth, which mutually contradict one another";[7] and this observation leads him to draw the skeptical moral that the human mind cannot hope to attain certainty about such deep questions—or at least, not of its own powers. The business of the Christian, he insists, is to be content with the truth which God has clearly revealed in the Scriptures; for it is only this truth which is certain and uncorrupted by human error and pride. Much more emphatically than Justin—and with the decisiveness of one who has not himself enjoyed the heady privilege of a philosophical education—Irenaeus repudiates both the content and the method of philosophy. If Irenaeus does make any constructive use of philosophical sources, therefore, it is most likely that he does so more or less unconsciously and at secondhand.

But abstract argument represents only one—and that not the most important—mode of Irenaeus's attack on Gnosticism. He mounts another, and from his point of view more crucial, assault: this time, upon the Gnostic claim to teach the authentic doctrine of Christ and the Apostles. We have seen that the Gnostics sought to show, by the allegorical exegesis of New Testament texts, how their mythology embodied the true, even if not the immediately obvious, meaning of these texts. They further supported this claim by the allegation that their doctrine was the secret teaching of Christ himself, which had been transmitted privately to the Apostles, and then handed on by them, in oral form, to Gnostic teachers. Taken together, these two assertions amounted to a claim that Gnosticism was the sole representative of the original and genuine Gospel message. They therefore raised in an acute form the questions of the authoritative sources of Christian teaching and of the criteria by which the authenticity of any particular doctrine was to be judged.

Irenaeus had, in reply, to establish both the historical and exegetical credentials of his own position.

This meant, in the first instance, that he had to demonstrate the agreement of his own anti-Gnostic Christianity with the teaching of Christ and the Apostles. To this end, he appeals to the inspired writings which were the basis of the Church's teaching. These included what were for him, as for the early Church generally, the Scriptures *par excellence:* the Septuagint version of the Jewish Bible. But they also included certain of the books of what later came to be called the New Testament: in particular, the four Gospels and the letters of St. Paul. These books, with the Acts of the Apostles, the Apocalypse, and certain of the other canonical epistles, Irenaeus cites as authoritative witnesses to that apostolic preaching which is the core of Christian belief. He insists that these written sources are the sole ultimate criterion of authentic Christian teaching.

Furthermore, he argues, the interpretation of these books cannot be made to depend upon an alleged "secret tradition," whose credentials are by hypothesis incapable of being tested. Whatever the Apostles taught, he insists, they taught publicly, for all Christians. They entrusted their wisdom not to unknown disciples, but to the men whom they set over the churches as their successors. Hence, the criterion for the understanding of the Scriptures is to be found in the openly proclaimed doctrine of those churches whose rulers have succeeded in publicly acknowledged order to the teaching office of the Apostles. This doctrine, Irenaeus maintains, is uniform throughout the Christian world. Furthermore, it is no esoteric mystery, but a simple declaration of that essential teaching which is the verifiable core of the scriptural message. If, then, the Gnostics claim that theirs is the authentic version of the Christian Gospel, they must show how it agrees with the Scriptures and with the Church's public Rule of Truth.

And this they cannot do—so Irenaeus, at great length, maintains. For the third level of his argument is essentially exegetical.

He takes the teachings of the prophets, of Christ as reported in the Gospels, and of the Apostles as their voices are heard in Acts and in the epistles; and he shows that what they say is directly contrary to the doctrine of his Gnostic opponents. This means, however, that in the course of his exegetical survey he develops, in clear if not systematic terms, what he takes to be the orthodox alternative to Gnosticism. In doing so, moreover, he makes use of exegetical and theological ideas which he has inherited from previous Christian writers, and from the Apologists in particular. Through these sources, if not directly, his understanding of the Scriptures is affected in a real measure by commonplace conceptions whose roots lie in the Greek philosophical tradition; and the importance of this influence is accentuated by the fact that the problems which his opposition to Gnosticism forces him to face are in many respects the same as those with which Greek philosophy had sought to cope. In this way, Irenaeus's elaboration of the alternative to Gnosticism draws him into the dialogue with Greek theological cosmology, whose conscious beginnings we have seen in the apologies of Justin.

THE UNITY AND TRANSCENDENCE OF GOD

Irenaeus's involvement in this dialogue is most easily seen in his attacks on the Gnostic doctrine of God and of God's relation to the world in creation and redemption. The issues raised by these problems compel him to discuss, directly or indirectly, the very questions which confronted Justin in his use of late Platonist ideas to interpret Christian teaching.

According to Irenaeus, there are two basic errors in the Gnostic picture of God. The first consists in a direct denial of his unity and uniqueness. Not only did the Gnostics separate the unknown Father of the Pleroma from the angelic Creator of the world, and thus postulate two parallel Gods at different "levels" of existence, they also multiplied deities at the level of the Pleroma itself, with their notion of gradations of Eons issuing from the supreme Father. In both ways, they called in question the essential biblical principle of monotheism. But more than this, they imposed a limitation either of power or of goodness on the supreme Father himself. For what else, Irenaeus asks, is implied by the Gnostic's insistence that the visible world was formed without the consent or interest of the Father? Was he so powerless that he could not stop—or at least control—this unhappy essay in creation? Or was he so indifferent that he did not care whether his ignorant understudy carried out the ill-conceived project or not? Either alternative, as Irenaeus hastens to point out, involves a denial of the majesty of God as the Scriptures understand it.

As against the Gnostics, therefore, Irenaeus affirms that God is one and unique in his majesty and goodness, and supreme in his power. The terms in which he sets these dogmas forth are drawn, interestingly enough, from Hellenistic Judaism and the theology of Middle Platonism. Thus, he writes that God is ingenerate, incomprehensible, without figure or shape, impassible, and incapable of error.[8] God is, as Plato rightly observed, incapable of being declared [9]—and therefore, as Irenaeus concludes in non-Platonic fashion, he is known only as he makes himself known. The Gnostics would thus do well to attend to the Scriptures in which God discloses himself. If they had done so,

they would have known clearly that God is not like men, and that his thoughts are not like the thoughts of men. For the Father of all things is far removed from those passions and affections which arise in men. He is simple and incomposite, of uniform nature throughout his being and absolutely like and equal to himself. For he is totally mind, and totally spirit, and totally intelligence, and totally thought, and totally reason, and totally hearing, and totally seeing, and totally light, and totally the source of all good things.[10]

This account of the transcendent mystery of God's nature emphasizes his difference from created things in terms which Justin or Albinus would have understood perfectly. But it combines with an insistence on the uniquely mysterious majesty of God a complementary affirmation, directed against the Gnostic picture of the Pleroma, that God's very nature is to be unanalyzably *one*.

But to this characterization of God, Irenaeus adds yet another note. He repeats over and again that God is *without limits*. The true God is himself the Pleroma, "the Fullness" of all things. As such, he is contained by nothing, yet himself contains whatever exists. Thus, he is unlimited both in his power and his presence: there is nothing apart from him and nothing which is not subject to him. In his unoriginate simplicity and eternity, God is the measureless context of all being, as well as its source: different from any creature, yet separated from none.

And just here it is impossible not to notice a significant difference between Irenaeus and Justin. For Justin, the chasm between generate and ingenerate existence, used to express the transcendence of the Creator over his creation, seems to imply a separation of the one from the other—a separation which is only overcome by the mediating agency of the Logos. Irenaeus, on the other hand, is combating, in Gnosticism, a teaching whose major emphasis is on the irreconcilability of divine Being with material existence. He is in search, therefore, of a way of asserting the transcendent majesty of God which will not seem to exclude him from the world. It is, in part, to this end that Irenaeus uses the notion of God's *limitlessness,* an idea which may well derive from Hellenistic Judaism. For what this notion means to him is not merely that God cannot be measured, but also that nothing sets a limit to his power and presence. What makes God *different* from every creature—his eternal and ingenerate simplicity—is thus, for Irenaeus, precisely what assures his direct and intimate *relation* with every creature. In this way, Irenaeus reaches for a solution to the problem which Justin had encountered when he defined the transcendence of God in terms of the opposition between Being and Becoming.

IRENAEUS AND THE LOGOS DOCTRINE

The characteristic note of Irenaeus's teaching about God can be seen clearly in his wrestlings with the Logos doctrine which he had inherited from the Apologists. He dutifully makes use of this doctrine: it was, after all, a settled part of the tradition which he had received. But he uses it only uncomfortably and with careful qualification.

Thus, we see Irenaeus employing Justin's idea of the Logos as Mediator. In one important passage, he reproduces a distinction between Father and Logos which directly reflects the Platonist distinction between the world-transcending supreme Mind and the immanent World Soul. The Father, he says, is "above all," whereas the Logos is "through all things." [11] The Word "in an invisible way contains everything which has been made and is immanent in the whole creation, because the Word of God guides and arranges all things." [12] Here the picture of divine transcendence is not unlike what we have already seen in Justin. The Father is somehow "outside" the world, and the Logos appears as an intermediate power through whom God is related to the world and works within it. Irenaeus can even hint at the idea, found also in Justin, that the Logos and the world are correlatives in the economy of divine creation. "For," he writes, "the Father sustains the creation and his own Logos at the same time." [13] Moreover, Irenaeus, like Justin, speaks of the Logos as the Mediator of revelation. The invisible and incomprehensible God is made known not directly, but through his Word: "The Son, administering all things for the Father, is active from the beginning even to the end, and apart from him no-one can know God. For the Son is the knowledge of the Father." [14] The language which Irenaeus uses in passages where he refers to this idea inevitably suggests the picture of God's relation to the world which we have seen Justin take over from Middle Platonism. The Word is the mode of the Father's relation to the generate world, from which God is himself separated by his very nature as the ingenerate source of all things.

In fact, however, Irenaeus's use of such language conceals a profound dissatisfaction with it. His opposition to Gnosticism makes him naturally averse to any conception which suggests either that there is more than one divine substance or that God is separated in some way from his world. As we have seen, his emphasis on the uniqueness and supremacy of God is combined with a corresponding distaste for the idea that God is not directly involved in his creation.

For these reasons, even though he uses the language of the Logos doctrine, Irenaeus quietly modifies certain of its implications. For example, he deliberately evades the issue of the "generation" of the Logos. Such language, all too reminiscent of Gnosticism, seems to suggest that the Word is a kind of halfway house between God and creation—a "derived" Deity; and this very idea is repellent to Irenaeus since it seems to presuppose divisions and distinctions of grade within the unique Godhead. At the same time, Irenaeus bends every effort to make it clear that the Logos is rightly, and not by some sort of equivocation, called "God." He is carefully distinguished from everything generate. Moreover, the action of the Logos, whether in creating or sustaining the world or in revealing the Father, is for Irenaeus the action of God himself. With the Spirit, the Word is one of the "hands" of God, whose creative activity *is* the immanent working of God.

Although he uses the language of the Logos theology as he had inherited it, Irenaeus attempts to overcome certain of the weaknesses which his opposition to Gnosticism compelled him to see in it. He tries to make of the Logos not a buffer between the ingenerate God and the generate world, but the presence within the world of the Godhead itself. The result of this attempt is, of course, a certain incoherence in his own position. His two ways of talking do not fit together very well; and the problem of how, or in what sense, the Logos was "generate" could not, as the future was to show, be evaded. Nevertheless, the tendency of Irenaeus's thought is plain enough. He has, in the face of Gnosticism, grasped more firmly than Justin what is involved in the idea of the uniqueness of God, and at the same time is seeking to reaffirm, in his inherited philosophical language, the active presence of the ingenerate God in and with the generate world.

THE DOCTRINE OF CREATION

These tendencies are confirmed by Irenaeus's treatment of the problem of creation. He follows Justin in adapting the distinction between generate and ingenerate existence to express the difference between Creator and creature. This distinction is, as we shall see, an important element in his thought. Yet, as we shall also see, he revises Justin's account significantly. The basis of his position we have already sketched. Faced with the Gnostic dualism which attempted to isolate the supreme God from the visible world, Irenaeus emphasizes repeatedly that God is the sole and direct author of the created order, which is the conscious work of his love and the object of his sustaining and redeeming activity. This doctrine, as he sees it, is the first essential article of that Rule of Truth which epitomizes the scriptural faith of the Church.

But it implies yet a further truth. To say that God is the sole and direct author of the generate world is to assert his absolute and unqualified responsibility for its being what it is. This in turn means that it is impious to think that in the creation God employed external instruments, intermediaries, or assistants. Even more obviously, it excludes the possibility that God's creative power was conditioned in any way by external circumstances. Irenaeus, therefore, formally repudiates the idea that creation can be understood as God's molding or shaping of a resistant "matter." This conception, as we have noted, was a commonplace of later Platonist theology, and was employed in effect to account for the factors of irrationality and instability in the material order. But Irenaeus could admit no such limitation on the power of God. Faced with the question of what the world is made and of what its material cause is, Irenaeus returns the straightforward answer, "Nothing." The world has no material cause. Its only cause is the absolute will of God, which called the world—"matter" included—into existence when before it had not been. "Men, indeed, are not able to make anything out of nothing, but only out of a material which lies to hand. But God is greater than men in this first regard, that he himself summoned into existence the material of his creation when before it had not been." [15]

And, of course, such a doctrine of creation—which was not original with Irenaeus[16]—implies a different view of the world itself as set over against its Creator. Irenaeus's vehement polemic against the Gnostic view of God and creation is all of a piece with his opposition to their characterization of the material world as intrinsically evil and alien from the divine Pleroma. Irenaeus's world is not alien from God. It is the expression of his goodness and the mirror of his will, a harmonious whole worthy of the Author who brought it into being. It is, therefore, good in all its parts, material as well as spiritual.

This attitude is nowhere more clear than in Irenaeus's insistence that all levels of created existence, material and spiritual alike, are subjects of divine redemption. For the Gnostic, redemption had two related meanings. In the first instance, and most narrowly, it involved the extrication of the "spirit" elements from the visible world and their restoration to the life of the Pleroma. In the largest sense, it meant a resegregation of the three components—body, soul, and spirit—which had got improperly intermingled in the formation of the world. In this view, of course, genuinely incorruptible life was the destiny only of that minority of men whose make-up included a spark of the divine substance. Irenaeus accepts the idea, by no means peculiar to the Gnostics, that redemption means sharing in incorruption—in the characteristics of ingenerate existence. But he insists that all men are created by God for this immortal kind of life; and furthermore, in the light both of his doctrine of creation and of the Christian idea of a resurrection of the body, he proclaims that it is the whole man, body as well as soul, which in Christ is elevated to a participation in the divine mode of existence. Thus, the world's essential goodness as the creature of God is confirmed and enhanced by its redemption through the incarnate Logos; and so far is the world from being alien to its Creator that it becomes in man the recipient of an immortal kind of life which is proper to God alone.

With this assertion—which he never tires of reiterating—Irenaeus does not merely set aside the Gnostic evaluation of the world-order. He also follows his predecessors in criticizing the Platonist idea that incorruptible life cannot belong to any part of the world of Becoming. This denial was, of course, based more on a definition than on an argument. The generate world of Becoming was regarded as intrinsically corruptible precisely because it consisted of the unstable and ephemeral elements in the world-system; and in Platonist ears, Christian talk of a redemption of the body must inevitably have sounded like talk of a round square. But Irenaeus supports the Christian view by appealing to the almighty power of God, who made the world in the first place out of nothing, and can therefore transform it as he will. The difference between Irenaeus's outlook and the viewpoint of a Platonist lies, therefore, not so much in their divergent estimates of the capacities of "body," as in their different ideas of the character of the world itself. In Irenaeus's eyes, the "nature" of things is not a system which includes God as its highest member, or one which, as a system, is independent of him and thus unchangeable. "Nature" is simply the expression of God's will; and, hence, if God proclaims his will that the bodies of men shall share in incorruption, there can be no question of his will being contrary to the "nature of things."

It *is* the nature of things. And that is the point at once of Irenaeus's doctrine of creation, and of his insistence on the intrinsic goodness and redeemability of the generate order.

THE PROBLEM OF EVIL

There is, however, an obvious difficulty in all this —and one which any Gnostic or Platonist would be bound to point out. Irenaeus offers no explanation of evil. He emphasizes the absolute power of God. He dwells on the goodness of God's creation. But if he really holds these opinions, why should he suppose that any "redemption" is necessary at all? What could go wrong in a world of the sort which he pictures? And if something has gone wrong, if a redemption is indeed necessary, how does he explain the fact? Irenaeus reports that this problem had been put to him in the form of a single question: "Could not God have manifested man as perfect from the beginning?" [17]

The Gnostic system had an immediate answer to this question. Indeed from one point of view, the Gnostic system simply *is* an answer to this question. The myth of Achamoth and the story of the Demiurge are both attempts to explain the origin of evil without imputing responsibility for it to the supreme Father. Furthermore, the theology of the *Timaeus* offers an equally direct and rather more credible solution of the same problem. In this case, the answer depends on the idea that the unstable nature of generate existence makes the full realization of rational order in the world impossible: or, in the language of Plato's myth, that the medium of "matter" is not wholly obedient to the hand of the divine Craftsman. This explanation of irrationality and disorder in the world therefore presupposes what Irenaeus cannot admit: an external limitation on the power of God. On the other hand, however, it does not impugn the goodness of the Craftsman, nor even seek to deny the relative goodness of the visible order itself. It merely suggests strongly that the intelligible world is a more proper habitat for immortal soul than is its material image.

And interestingly enough, it is an adapted form of the Platonist answer which Irenaeus himself propounds. His solution depends for its credibility on the connotations of the division between generate and ingenerate existence. But it adjusts this distinction both to a Christian idea of creation and to a Christian view of the significance of the world as an historical order.

The key to Irenaeus's solution lies in the simple idea that there is *one* limitation on the power of God which cannot be denied. When God creates, the product of his action cannot be an uncreated thing. This, be it noted, is not a limitation imposed on God by some external condition, such as the existence of a refractory "matter." It is a limitation of a *logical* order. That created things should be uncreated is a logical, not a physical, impossibility; and it is therefore an impossibility which not even the power of God can overcome.

But to say that something is "created" means that it is not, like God, ingenerate and eternal, but that it is generate: intrinsically changeable and corruptible. In his description of what it means to be a creature, Irenaeus applies epithets which are drawn from Platonist accounts of the nature of Becoming. Thus, he explains that creatures are things which "had a beginning, and are capable of dissolution . . . and stand in need of him who made them." [18] Since they are not, like God, ingenerate, it follows that of their own nature creatures are imperfect, and therefore subject to growth and its contrary, decay. Hence, Irenaeus writes, it makes no sense to ask why God did not make man perfect from the beginning. For since men are not "ingenerate, for this very reason they fall short of perfection." [19]

Here, then, is the explanation of evil, and with it of man's need of redemption. As a finite creature, whose will lacks discipline and stability as his mind lacks knowledge, man uses his freedom to disobey God, and thus falls away from his Creator into sin. This is not God's fault. It is the fault of man, whose freedom effects what his limitations as a creature make possible.

Although God cannot create man already perfect, he can remedy both man's sin and his natural limitations. He can bring his creature gradually to a higher level of existence; and this, as Irenaeus sees it, is precisely the meaning of the history of mankind. The omnipotence of God first creates, and then perfects what has been created.

> Man must first of all come to be; and once existing, he must grow; and having grown, he must be strengthened; and having been strengthened, he must be multiplied; and having multiplied, he must be confirmed; and having been confirmed, he must be glorified; and having been glorified, he must see his Lord. For it is God whom he is to see. But the vision of God brings about incorruption; and incorruption effects nearness to God.[20]

Thus, the end of this process is man's entrance upon a life which is no longer subject to the limitations of generate existence: a life in which, in fact, the liabilities of creaturehood are overcome by the grace of God. This life is characterized by that incorruption which both results from and leads to the vision of God and the mirroring of God's glory in man himself.

So it is that the inevitable imperfection of a generate world provides Irenaeus with an explanation of evil which seems to him consistent with the power and goodness of God. Evil is rooted not in some sort of cosmic "opposition party," but in the necessary nature of created existence: its weakness, instability, and (in rational beings) ignorance. It is these circumstances which make man's power of self-determination an occasion of sin, and thus provide the necessary, if not the sufficient, condition of his alienation from God. The world which God creates is unavoidably a world of Becoming and not of Being. Hence, it is a world in which the occurrence of error and sin is not merely possible but probable.

But Irenaeus sees this generate world with the eyes of a biblical exegete, not with those of a natural philosopher. That is to say, he does not see it as an unalterable natural order, but as an evolving historical process, guided by the providence of its Creator. For this reason, the finitude and imperfection of both soul and body in man do not seem to him an occasion for resignation or despair. Rather he sees them as the presupposition of man's historical redemption, which provides both a remedy for sin and a cure for corruptibility. By the same token, that immortal and Godlike character, which for the Platonist is a given and permanent aspect of the soul's natural constitution, becomes for Irenaeus the goal of the history of salvation, the realization of God's purpose in creation. In a word, Irenaeus employs a Platonist understanding of the finitude of the empirical order as a framework for his exposition of the meaning of the scriptural history of God's dealings with men. Through his Word, God creates the world. He then reveals himself to Moses and the prophets. Finally, he fulfills the promise of these earlier redemptive actions in the summary and culminating event of the Incarnation; and each of these events is a step in the process by which God realizes for his creature that purpose which was originally declared when he made him "in the image of God." The end of the process is the overcoming of mortality, error, and sin through the free gift of God's grace.

This scheme exhibits what is perhaps the classical statement of Christian belief in terms of the problems and conceptions native to the rational theology of the Greeks. It may seem ironical, or even paradoxical, that the author of this scheme should be a man whose attitude toward Greek philosophy varied only from indifference to hostility—and one who, moreover, seems to have lacked all but the rudiments of a philosophical education. But in reality, these facts only make his achievement the more credible. Irenaeus was not troubled, as a person more learned in philosophical matters might have been, by the specific problems which arose out of the confrontation of Christian preaching and Greek philosophy. Indeed, for him, since he rarely makes conscious or positive use of philosophical sources, there was no such confrontation. There was only the problem of constructing, out of the diverse materials provided by his scriptural and theological heritage, a defensively elaborated statement of the content of the Church's Rule of Faith.

From these sources, he draws his conception of the world as a historical process expressive of the righteous purposes of God. From these sources, he draws his faith in the Word-made-Flesh as the consummation of God's redemptive activity. And from the same sources again, he draws his conviction that the meaning of this history is to be found in man's passage from a generate to an incorruptible form of existence, from alienation to fellowship with the ingenerate God. Without any clear notion of what he is doing, Irenaeus thus takes a basic idea of the Platonist theology, with the wealth of religious connotation attaching to it, and applies it not as a tool for analyzing the order of nature, but as a key for understanding the course of history.

ACHIEVEMENTS AND PROBLEMS

How useful or successful was this scheme? There can be no doubt that it provided for the future a kind of outline-sketch of a Christian world-picture, or that in its basic lineaments it gave a shape to much of later Christian thought. And the reasons for this are not far to seek.

Most notably, Irenaeus's scheme completes in principle the intellectual transformation by which "generate existence" comes to connote "existence in absolute dependence upon God"—a transformation which in Justin's thought was only inadequately carried out. But this achievement is closely related to other aspects of Irenaeus's thought. For one thing, it seems to be this idea which provides the key to Irenaeus's way of dealing with the problem of God's transcendence. His conception of God as intimately and directly involved in the world, yet "beyond" it in virtue of the mode of his being, owes much to the fact that Irenaeus understands the majesty of God precisely in terms of his relation to the world as its absolute Lord.

Another equally important consequence of Irenaeus's interpretation of "generate existence" is his sense that the "nature" of things simply *is* what God purposes to make of them, and not a character which is independent of God's will. On the basis of this conception, Irenaeus can think of human history as a process whose end is a state of affairs significantly different from its beginning precisely because, for him, to be "generate" means to be totally dependent upon God and therefore open to his continuing creative activity. By the same token, it makes sense in this view of things for Irenaeus to talk of a redemption and transformation of the *body,* and to suppose that material existence is not by its "nature" alien to God.

In all these ways, Irenaeus's scheme seemed to offer an acceptable Christian reading and revision of a late Platonic world-picture. But this does not mean that it was either wholly coherent or universally applauded in the form in which Irenaeus propounded it. For example, it offered no real solution of the standing problem of the status of the Logos. From yet another point of view, Irenaeus's attempt to solve the problem of evil by an appeal to creaturely finitude raised a whole host of questions and difficulties—as even Irenaeus, in his own way, seems to have realized. Was his solution to be taken as asserting that sin is simply a matter of "nature"? Surely not. But if this is *not* what it meant, then does it really offer a solution at all? These issues were to preoccupy Christian thinkers for centuries; and the future was to show that Irenaeus's suggested solution could not satisfy everyone.

Notes to Chapter III

1. Acts 8:9 f.
2. *AH* I. Praef. 2.
3. *AH* I.2.4.
4. *AH* III.25.5.
5. *AH* II.14.2.
6. *Ibid.*
7. *AH* II.27.1.
8. *AH* II.12.1.
9. *AH* IV.6.3.
10. *AH* II.13.3.
11. *AH* V.18.2.
12. *AH* V.18.3.
13. *AH* V.18.2.
14. *AH* IV.6.7.
15. *AH* II.10.4.
16. See *Hermas, Mand.* I.1; and Theophilus of Antioch, *Ad Autol.* II.10, cf. II.4.
17. *AH* IV.38.1.
18. *AH* III.8.3.
19. *AH* IV.38.1.
20. *AH* IV.38.3.

CHAPTER IV. *Tertullian –*
A Latin Perspective

WE TURN from Irenaeus, the Greek-speaking bishop of Gaulish Lyons, to Tertullian, the Latin-speaking lawyer and presbyter of Carthage, in North Africa. This ought, in principle, to be an easy and natural transition. Chronologically speaking, Tertullian's career as a Christian took up roughly where Irenaeus's left off. The African was doubtless acquainted with the great *Adversus Haereses;* and if so, one can be sure that he read it with no little sympathy, since doctrines of the sort which it attacked were a familiar problem to him, and were to elicit some of his own most trenchant writing. Moreover, Tertullian was the conscious disciple of Irenaeus's predecessors, the apologists; and in particular, perhaps, of Justin Martyr, whose address to Antoninus he imitated and surpassed in his own brilliant *Apology*. The reader might expect, therefore, as he turned to Tertullian, to find in his numerous writings a further development of the lines of thought which we have traced in earlier writers.

This expectation is not disappointed. But it is fulfilled in an odd and paradoxical way, for Tertullian represents something of a new strain as a Christian thinker. A rhetorician and a lawyer by profession, he was not only the first Christian theologian to write in Latin but also the first Christian theologian whose natural intellectual milieu was that of later Roman Stoicism. In-

99

deed, Tertullian was a child of Rome in more ways than one. This meant, of course, that he was also an admirer of the Greeks, since the Latin intelligentsia had for a long time been students and imitators of Greek culture. But if Tertullian shares with such Latin authors as Cicero and Seneca their respect for Greek thought, he also shares their distinctive interest in the problem of a historical human society which will fulfill the divine will for man.

In Tertullian's case, however, these attitudes are transformed and qualified by his Christian faith. The "Greek" thought whose insights he values and seeks to interpret is primarily that of his Greek Christian predecessors; and the society in whose mission he sees man's destiny foreshadowed is not the Augustan Empire, with its center in Rome, but the Christian Church, with its historical roots in the apostolic community at Jerusalem. Tertullian is indeed a Roman; but a *Christian* Roman.

Both his Christianity and his Latin outlook, however, are further conditioned by his own temperamental peculiarities. As a Christian, Tertullian was a convert; as a Roman, he was a colonial. Almost inevitably, then, his writings reflect the harsh enthusiasm, passionate idealism, and fierce loyalty of one who is somehow bound to be purer than the pure. Tertullian thus brings his wit, his epigrammatic style, and his dialectical skills into the service of an attitude which can see only two sides of every question—the clearly right, and the absolutely wrong; and which further can be satisfied with nothing less than absolute practical commitment to the right. In matters of theology, as well as morals, Tertullian is a rigorist, quite beyond any thought of compromise or accommodation. It was this mentality which encouraged him, at the height of his career, to join the heretical Montanist movement, and even, at the end, to found his own sect within it.

It is of no use, therefore, to discuss the thought of Tertullian, or to consider the way he treats the problems of theological cosmology, without first taking account of his own distinctive way of conceiving the issues which confronted him. For even though the materials of his theology are almost slavishly taken over from the tradition which he had received, their meaning *for him* is materially affected by his particular point of view, background, and temperament. His conception of the nature and sources of Christian theology; his attitude toward pagan philosophy; his own philosophical predilections; above all his peculiar understanding of the human problem for which he seeks an answer in Christian faith—all these factors influence the way in which he uses his theological heritage, and the way in which he conceives and formulates the question of God in his relation to the world.

CHRISTIANITY AS REVELATION

Tertullian attaches as much significance as Irenaeus to the identification and preservation of authentic apostolic Christianity. He, too, sees the faith in a situation of peril, not merely from the Roman State but also from heretical movements whose teaching threatened to adulterate and deform the truth which had been entrusted to the Church. Irenaeus had been compelled by the threat to his flock to compose a vast treatise against Gnosticism. Tertullian was impelled to write not only against the Gnostics but also against the perverse Paulinism of Marcion, against the "monarchianism" or unitarian views of certain teachers in Rome, and against the quasi-Platonist dualism of a man called Hermogenes. He was aware, therefore, of manifold threats to Christian teaching; and these threats stimulated him, as they had stimulated Irenaeus, to define external criteria for the authentic doctrine of Christ.

The basis of Tertullian's position is the principle that the Christian faith has as its content a revealed doctrine. This idea was certainly not new with him; but in his writings, it assumes an explicit and formal role. To be "wise in the things of God," he thinks, it is not enough to have that common-sense belief in Deity which is the universal conviction of mankind. For God in a Christian view is not a lifeless block who waits for human ingenuity and insight to search him out. God himself makes himself known—and this supremely in Christ, in whom he has chosen to be both known and worshiped. Tertullian therefore inveighs against those who make up a God or a religion for themselves. The wise man is the one who "acts in accordance with, not in opposition to, the divine dispensation";[1] and true religion is that faith which responds obediently to God's self-revelation, which acknowledges and honors God by believing and doing what he has revealed of his will. This principle is the essential basis of all that Tertullian teaches.

If one asks what the source of this revealed doctrine is, Tertullian is quite clear. It is in what has been written—in the Jewish Scriptures and "the evangelical and apostolic writings" [2] —that the Christian seeks his knowledge of God and of God's will. The significance which Tertullian attaches to the Scriptures can be estimated both from his words and from his practical procedures in theological debate. Of the sectaries against whom he writes, Tertullian makes only one demand: that they prove their case from the sacred writings. Moreover, he himself follows the rule which he thus advocates for others. His solutions for the problems which he discusses are invariably based in the first instance on exegesis of relevant biblical texts. Hence, the greater part of his lengthy work against Marcion of Pontus is an extended interpretation of the Gospel according to St. Luke, the one Gospel whose authority Marcion was prepared to acknowledge; and his work on the doctrine of creation, against the mysterious Hermogenes, depends upon an exegesis of the opening words of Genesis.

But Tertullian faced the same problem in regard to the Scriptures as Irenaeus had faced. The heretics could also interpret the Scriptures; and the question was bound to arise, whose interpretation was the correct one? This question could, of course, be settled in detail by careful consideration of text after text. Such argument, however, was both wearisome and, for simple people who had neither the time nor the learning to follow it, profitless. Tertullian therefore evolved, not without the help of Irenaeus's precedent, a "short way" with heretics.[3] His argument was, in effect, that the teaching of the heretics, unlike that of the Church's universal Rule of Faith, could neither trace its lineage back to the Apostles, nor command the present common assent of the churches. These two facts, he thought, added up to an initial presumption against the truth of the heretical teachings—a presumption, that is to say, against their authenticity as parts of the doctrine which God has revealed.

"A heretic," Tertullian writes, "may . . . be designated as one who, forsaking that which was prior, afterwards chose out for himself that which did not exist in times past." [4] By contrast, the unanimous faith of the churches is "that Rule . . . which the churches have transmitted from the Apostles, the Apostles from Christ, and Christ from God." [5] Everyone knows, Tertullian argues, that Marcion's God was first announced in the reign of Antoninus.[6] But this was more than 115 years after Christ. How, then, can Marcion, against the unanimous witness of the churches whose confession dates back to the Apostles, maintain that his is the true Christian and scriptural teaching? His views are ruled out before argument by their inconsistency with apostolic tradition in the form of the Rule of Faith, and by their dissociation from the paradigmatic teaching of the Church in its apostolic origins.

If, then, a man is looking for the truth about God's revealed will, the ultimate source of the knowledge which he seeks must be the Scriptures. Its proximate source will be the Church's Rule of Faith, which embodies the authentic meaning of the Scriptures in a form guaranteed both by its historical origins and by the common assent of the churches throughout the world.

To be a Christian, as Tertullian understands it, is precisely to be obedient to this Rule, to the doctrine and the way of life made known by God. "Faith consists in a rule; it has its law, and finds its well-being in the observance of that law." [7] This Rule is not only necessary but sufficient. Nothing may be believed against it, and nothing need be known in addition to it. Tertullian holds no brief for theological speculation or for pointless diggings into the dark corners of Scripture. Seeking, he points out, must come to an end when the truth is known.[8] The Rule —the doctrine of God made known in Christ—is the truth which men seek when they search for God and his will. Hence, the business of life is not to expand the Rule, to change it, or to play unnecessary intellectual variations on it, but simply to keep and defend it. And this, Tertullian conceives to be his theological task.

THE STATUS OF PHILOSOPHY

In the light of this position, it is easy enough to imagine what Tertullian's attitude was toward Greek philosophy. From his point of view, it represented a competitor and not an ally of Christian faith. This was not so much because its exponents invariably taught falsehood, but because its approach to the mysteries of religion was exactly that of "seeking" and of speculation, rather than that of faith in the divinely revealed content of Scripture. The philosopher in his search for God relies on human wisdom; and the one result of his confidence in this weak instrument is the fostering of a multiplicity of discordant opinions and sects, amongst which the truth is lost. What most distresses Tertullian, however, is not the fact, already dwelt upon by such writers as Justin and Irenaeus, that philosophers disagree among themselves, but the fact that the introduction of the speculative mood among Christians has occasioned the proliferation of sects, "opinions," and divisions even among the faithful. He points out that St. Paul long ago had warned the Colossians against "philosophy." [9] The Apostle's own experience had set him on guard against human wisdom; and his experience, Tertullian avers, has only been confirmed by that of the churches after him. The philosophers have turned out to be the "patriarchs of heresy." [10] Platonism is the source of Valentinian Gnosticism.[11] Stoicism is the real originator of Marcion's God.[12] "Take away . . . from the heretics the wisdom they share with the heathen, and let them support their inquiries from the Scriptures alone: they will be unable to keep their ground." [13]

Tertullian thus sees in philosophy an alien influence, a source of attitudes and ideas which corrupt the Rule of Faith. "What has Athens to do with Jerusalem, the Academy with the Church, the heretics with the Christians? Our teaching derives from the Stoa of Solomon, who himself transmitted the principle that God must be sought in simplicity of heart. Of what importance is it, then, that there are men who have set forth a 'Stoic' and a 'Platonic' and a 'dialectical' Christianity? We for our part have no need of curiosity now that we have found Jesus Christ, and no need of searching after we have found the Gospel." [14] Greek philosophy, as Tertullian sees it, is not merely a set or sets of opinions. It is a historically identifiable tradition of thought embodied in a continuing series of human communities which perpetuate the original teaching of their founders. And Christianity necessarily stands outside this tradition. For Christianity is, in fact, itself *another* tradition, living on in a distinct community, the Church, and perpetuating not the views of Plato or Aristotle, but the revealed teaching of God himself. The Gospel is therefore an *alternative* to philosophy, and its truth can only be preserved when it is kept free from adulteration with the principles of any rival tradition.

Tertullian's hostility to philosophy does not extend to all the specific teachings of individual philosophers. He can approve of Plato's views on the immortality of the soul,[15] and his admiration for Seneca, the first-century Roman Stoic, is often cited as an indication that his repudiation of philosophy was not thoroughgoing. He even repeats Justin's theory that the philosophers borrowed some of their ideas from the Jewish Scriptures,[16] and this theory seems, as we have remarked, to presuppose certain rudimentary agreements between philosophers and Christians.

Moreover, Tertullian's hostility to the speculations of philosophers is not an attack on what modern thinkers have called "natural theology." Tertullian does not for one moment doubt that man may come to a true, if inadequate, knowledge of God apart from the revelation given through the prophets and through Christ. He even specifies two distinct ways in which such knowledge is available (both of which reflect commonplaces of the Stoic philosophy of his day). The first way is, in Tertullian's words, "from God's works": that is, from the order and beauty of the visible cosmos.[17] It is supplemented and reinforced by "the testimony of the soul itself, which, though confined by the prison of the body, though limited by bad education, though enervated by its passions and desires, though forced to serve false gods, nevertheless, when it comes to itself . . . names God by this name only, because it is the proper name of the true God." [18] Here, Tertullian appeals in effect to the Stoic doctrine of "common notions" [19]—ideas universally and uniformly produced by human experience. One such idea is that of God, whose reality is thus acknowledged, not as the result of a conscious chain of reasoning, but by the immediate testimony of the soul, which, Tertullian says, is "naturally Christian." [20]

The revelation which is given in the Scriptures as the rule of Christian faith thus has the common, if frequently inarticulate, conviction of the whole human race to build upon. But Tertullian—though his account of the sources of this conviction reveals his wholly natural acceptance of certain Stoic ideas—does not want to confuse the natural knowledge of God with the result of philosophical speculation. If anything, philosophy succeeds, he thinks, only in introducing confusion and distortion into a knowledge which is the natural endowment of every man. It is Christian faith which clarifies, articulates, and completes this knowledge. Even though the philosophers may from time to time have hit upon truth; even though their speculation is itself built upon the foundation of a natural belief in God; nevertheless, in their hands the truth becomes a matter of debate and dispute. It is clouded over with the uncertainties of controversy.

Against this confusion stands the revealed Rule of Faith. It does not, Tertullian admits, answer all speculative questions. But it does in fact, directly or by implication, answer the most important of them: questions about God, the world, the soul, and the relations among them. And it is these answers which Tertullian seeks to expound in his theological writings. He makes use of the Scriptures and of the tradition of Christian thought, as he had received it, to explain, illustrate, and defend the revealed alternative to the confusions of the philosophers and heretics.

THE CONTENT OF THE RULE

What, then, did this Rule of Faith contain? The answer to this question is important, not merely in itself but also because, in the light of what we have said about Tertullian's attitude toward the Rule, it affords a crucial clue for the understanding of his attitude toward the theological cosmology of his Christian predecessors.

In his shortest summary of the Rule, it includes just three items: belief in one sole God, the Creator of the universe; belief in Jesus Christ, born of the Virgin Mary and Son of the Creator-God; and belief in the resurrection of the flesh.[21] Obviously, however, he regards these heads of belief as capable of expansion. In another passage he writes:

The Rule of Faith . . . is that whereby it is believed that there is only one sole God, who is none other than the Founder of the world; who brought the world out of nothing through his Word, who was sent forth the first of all things: that this Word, called God's Son, appeared in the name of God in various ways to the patriarchs, was heard at all times in the speaking of the prophets, and finally, by the Spirit and Power of God his Father, was brought down into the Virgin Mary, made flesh in her womb, and, born of her, lived as Jesus Christ: that he then preached a new law and a new promise of the Kingdom of Heaven, that he did wonders, that he was crucified, that he rose on the third day, that he was taken into heaven and sits on the right hand of the Father; that he sent in his place the power of the Holy Spirit to lead believers; that he will come in glory to bring the saints into eternal life and the fruition of the celestial promises, and to condemn the wicked to eternal fire, after the resurrection of both groups and the resurrection of their flesh.[22]

This much longer formulation is still further modified in the treatise *Against Praxeas*,[23] where Tertullian introduces expressions to define a doctrine of the Trinity and to specify the nature of the incarnate Word. Obviously, the content of the Rule is, within limits, variable. It includes, apart from certain basic elements of Christian proclamation, other items of strictly theoretical import which Tertullian thinks are a plain part of the tradition and which are relevant to the issues he is currently discussing.

These items, however, are worthy of particular notice. They amount to an abbreviated summary of the central ideas of that theological world-picture whose earlier development we have traced in the writings of Justin and Irenaeus. Thus, Tertullian refers to the doctrine of the unique God who is related to the world-order as its Creator. He insists upon the dogma that the world was created "out of nothing"; and he identifies the Son of God as the Logos who was generated from the Father to be the Mediator in creation and redemption. We have already seen how this constellation of ideas was evolved, interpreted, and defined in the context of a dialogue between Christian teaching and the religious cosmology of the Hellenistic world. What must be noted here is that Tertullian gives this set of interrelated conceptions a place among the structural elements of scriptural doctrine. In his eyes they are, in a word, dogma. He sees them quite simply as Christian ideas which are a given part of the apostolic tradition; and in his own exposition of them, he treats them as such. That is, he reiterates and defends them, in the form in which he had received them, as the direct teaching of the revealed deposit of faith.

This discussion directly suggests two conclusions. It appears, first of all, that we may expect to find reproduced in Tertullian's writings the essentials of the Christianized Platonist world-picture which he inherited from his predecessors. But further, we may expect to find that Tertullian reiterates these ideas because, and insofar as, he sees them as constituent elements in the Rule of Faith, or, in other words, we may expect to find that he repeats without reconsidering. Let us see whether these preliminary conclusions fit the facts.

THE DOCTRINE OF CREATION

Take first the fundamental problem of the relation between God and the world: the issue of creation. Tertullian deals explicitly with this problem in his treatise *Against Hermogenes*. Here he attacks the position of one "who will not have it that [God] made all things out of nothing." [24] Hermogenes, he reports, "premises that the Lord made all things either out of Himself, or out of nothing, or out of something: in order that, when he has shown that He could not have made them either out of Himself or out of nothing, he may then affirm the remaining alternative, that God made them out of something, and therefore that that something was matter." [25] Tertullian's own view, of course, is that which we have seen Irenaeus adopt: "What we worship is the only God, who by his Word . . . drew out of nothing, for the glorification of his majesty, this whole immense system." [26] As against Hermogenes, Tertullian supports this argument by adducing two kinds of argument.

The most elaborately developed of these is exegetical in character. Hermogenes had apparently argued that the creation narrative in Genesis supported his own position. He took it that the "beginning" in which God is said to have created the heavens and the earth was precisely the "matter" out of which the world was made, and that a further allusion to a pre-existing matter might be seen in the mention of "the earth" as "without form and void." [27] Tertullian—who sees in Hermogenes' position nothing more than an attempt to substitute a form of Platonism for the teaching of the Bible—refutes these contentions at great length. He points out that the "beginning," or "principle," (the Greek word *arché* has both meanings) of God's creation is not matter, but God's Wisdom, or Word, through whom all things were made. The word "earth," furthermore, does not mean formless matter, but the first of the four elements. Scripture, in fact, does not use the word "matter," and in any case does not mention anything "out of which" the world was made. For Tertullian, the conclusion is inevitable: "If the material is not mentioned, while the work and the Maker of the work are both mentioned, it is manifest that he made the work out of nothing." [28] Thus, the Scriptures, though only by their silence, are clear that God is no Demiurge who fashions a world-order out of some recalcitrant stuff, but the absolute Lord, who by his Word summons the universe into existence when before it did not exist at all.

Tertullian's second form of argument consists in pointing out the absurd consequences for a doctrine of God which follow if Hermogenes' position is accepted. The Rule of Faith, says Tertullian (and we may compare the teaching of Justin and Irenaeus), lays it down that "nothing except God is ingenerate." [29] God alone excepted, therefore, everything which exists is both changeable and perishable; and this very fact argues that it is only God who is eternal and without beginning. But if one assumes that there has always coexisted with God a "stuff" out of which he made the world, then the unique majesty of God is denied: he is not the "sole ingenerate," but shares his glory with something else. This, however, is an impossible conclusion. "God must be single because God is the supreme. But the only thing which is supreme is that which is unique; and nothing can be unique which has anything equal to it." [30] Thus, the doctrine of creation out of nothing, for Tertullian as for Irenaeus, is a guarantee of the unique majesty of God, and its contrary a derogation from his majesty.

GOD AND HIS TRANSCENDENCE

Implicit, therefore, in Tertullian's defense of the doctrine of creation is a view of the nature and transcendence of God: a spelling out of what the Rule of Faith means when it says that there is one sole God, the Creator. It is, Tertullian argues, the mark of Deity to be *eternal:* that is, to be ingenerate, uncreated, without beginning or end.[31] He uses epithets of this sort, and expounds them, in passage after passage, marking the transcendence and majesty of God by use of the traditional Greek contrast of stable and immortal existence with existence which is unstable and possesses nothing permanently or in its own right. Tertullian, like Irenaeus and Justin, formally equates this distinction with that between the Creator and his works, and thus uses it to define the uniqueness of the Christian God.

Accordingly, he dwells on the facts that God is invisible and incomprehensible, in a fashion sometimes reminiscent of the spirit of Albinus. "What makes God comprehensible," he writes, "is the fact that he cannot be comprehended, so that the very power of his greatness presents him to men as at once known and unknown." [32] The inability of the human mind to grasp God is based on the fact that God is, in the last resort, *unlike* anything in the generate world.[33] He is measureless, and therefore can only be known fully to himself.[34]

Unique in his ingeneracy, this infinite God is also superior to time and change. To describe the character of God's eternity, Tertullian resorts in one place to language which is redolent of Platonism. "Eternity," he writes, "has no time. It is itself all time.

It acts; it cannot then suffer. It cannot be born, therefore it lacks age. . . . God . . . is as independent of beginning and end as he is of time." [35] God, then, is timeless and impassible. Tertullian even goes so far as to say in one passage—though only with the addition of embarrassed qualifications—that God is immutable.[36]

There can be no doubt, then, that Tertullian accepts the Platonized doctrine of God and creation which he had inherited from his predecessors as normative Christian teaching. Sometimes he is troubled by its apparent implications: as by the doctrine of divine immutability, which tends to grate on his conviction that the God of the Bible is anything but "inactive and listless." [37] Nevertheless, in spite of his occasional doubts and his deliberate policy of preferring scriptural to philosophical language, he faithfully reproduces the ideas which his sources had used, and sets them forth as having the authority of orthodox tradition. It is, therefore, all the more puzzling to note that he seems not to have understood, or at any rate not to have come to terms with, the philosophical presuppositions of the theology he transmits.

TERTULLIAN'S MATERIALISM

There is, for example, every reason to think that Tertullian conceived of Deity in the classical Stoic fashion: that is to say, as an impalpable corporeal substance which in some sense occupies space. There is a hint of this idea in a curious argument which Tertullian puts forth in the first book of *Against Marcion,* where he is arguing against the possibility of there being a second God.

Since . . . the universe belongs to the Creator, I see no room for any other God. All things are full of their Author, and occupied by him. If in created beings there be any portion of space anywhere void of Deity, obviously what it is empty of is a false God.[38]

The suggestion of this argument is that God fills all space—and *not* merely in the sense that his presence is real in every place because he is beyond spatial limits and categories.

But this is not all. Tertullian speaks explicitly in a number of passages of God's "substance" being "spirit," and he defines "spirit" as "a special kind of body." [39] This idea is a direct borrowing of the Stoic teaching that the Divine is a "fiery spirit" which permeates and animates the world: a teaching which in principle makes nonsense of the Platonist conception of a God transcendent, immaterial, and exempt from the categories of space and time. Tertullian, with no sense of the incompatibility of these two ways of thinking of God, sets them side by side, using ideas drawn from both in turn to interpret the data of the scriptural revelation. No doubt there is a fairly obvious explanation of how he came to follow this procedure. Tertullian took over one way of thinking about God from the theological tradition which he had received: a tradition whose content he associated with the authority of the Rule of Faith. The other way of thinking represents his own habit of mind, one which he no doubt acquired in the process of his education, in circles where a Latinized Stoicism was prevalent. But such an explanation does nothing to solve the basic problem of the inconsistency in his thought.

TERTULLIAN AND THE LOGOS

The problem is illustrated by Tertullian's treatment of the idea of the Logos. Here again, his fundamental intent is to reproduce the orthodox teaching of his predecessors. Accordingly, we find that he employs the same set of terminological equations as had been used earlier by Justin and others—equations which, as we have seen, reflect the influence on Christian thought of both Hellenized Judaism and late Platonism. The Son of God, Tertullian explains, is God's *Logos*, that is (as he points out for the benefit of his Latin-speaking readers), God's Reason and God's Word. He is also that Wisdom of God which is mentioned in the Book of Proverbs,[40] and that Spirit of God which St. Paul says "knows the things of God." [41] It is, Tertullian says, this Spirit which animates the world, just as it is this Reason which "put the universe together out of a diversity of elements." [42] The Logos, then, is the divine power which informs and governs the cosmic order, just as he is "the maker of the universe," [43] the "hand of God." [44] Distinct from the Father, he is the Father's agent in creation and the one through whom the Father is revealed to men. Tertullian thus accepts Justin's mediatorial idea of the Logos. He distinguishes between the Father and the Word as between one who is essentially invisible and one who may be seen by men. "By him who is invisible, we must understand the Father in the fullness of his majesty, while we recognize the Son as visible by reason of the dispensation of his derived existence." [45]

Here are all the elements of the classical Logos theology, which Tertullian takes over without obvious criticism, and without Irenaeus's acute sense of discomfort. For Tertullian as for Justin, the Logos is intrinsically connected with the *world*, manifesting in it and for it the creative and redemptive will of the transcendent Father. Tertullian underlines this correlation of Logos and world by speaking of the Word of God as "generate" and even as "created." "The . . . Wisdom of God is declared to be generated and created, for the especial reason that we should not suppose that there is any other being than God alone who is ingenerate and uncreated. . . . His Wisdom . . . was then generated and created when in the mind of God it began to be stirred up for the arrangement of his creative works." [46] The same idea—that the Logos appears or is generated as a distinct "thing" in connection with the creation of the world—appears in the treatise *Against Praxeas*. There, Tertullian explains that the Logos first existed *in God* as his Reason, and was then "made a second" to God, or "uttered," as the Word by which the world was made.[47] This theory of the "two states" of the Logos, which Tertullian took over from the apologists, emphasizes both the secondary and mediatorial character of the Logos, and his essential relatedness to the world-order.

But here Tertullian comes face to face with the classical problem of the status of the Logos. Is the Word to be conceived as a second and inferior God? Is he a sort of halfway house between ingenerate Being and the material order of Becoming? And if so, what becomes of Christian monotheism, or of the Church's traditional insistence upon the uniqueness of God? Irenaeus had sought to answer these questions by decrying speculation about the "generation" of the Logos. Tertullian is bolder. He meets the problem head-on. But he meets it by reiterating the sort of solution which had been suggested by Justin, recast in the light of his own idea that God is a quasi-corporeal "spirit."

Thus, he explains, first of all, that there is a difference between the Logos and other things which are labeled "generate and created." The Logos is not brought into being out of nothing. Rather, he is a "derivation and portion" [48] of the Father's divine substance. Hence, he is neither independent of the Father nor a different kind of being from the Father. There is only one Deity—only one divine "substance." But this divine substance is, so to speak, articulated. Without loss of its essential nature, it exists in an original and a derived form. God, writes Tertullian, "sent forth the Word . . . just as the root puts forth the tree, and the fountain the river, and the sun its ray. . . . But still the tree is not severed from the root, nor the river from the fountain, nor the ray from the sun; nor indeed, is the Word separated from God." [49] There are not two or three Gods, then. For the divine substance—that "spirit" which is the peculiar stuff of Deity—is the same in Father, Word, and Paraclete. But the Father is the fullness of Deity, whereas the Logos is a secondary derivation of that fullness.

In principle, then, Tertullian does not deviate from the theology of the apologists. He merely explains it. But he explains it in a way which reveals a failure on his part to grasp the logic of the problem, created as it was by the attempt to assimilate biblical monotheism to an essentially Platonist world-picture. To answer the question of how Deity can be "generate," he appeals to the Stoic idea of a divine "stuff," which is somehow shared or stretched out. This answer satisfies him. But it does so, and can do so, only because of the special form which his interest in the question takes. He does not address himself to the substantive question of how it is possible to speak of a derived, or secondary, Deity in a view which conceives of the one God as uniquely "ingenerate." Rather, he sets out to construct an apology for a theology which does just this; and he achieves his purpose by appealing to a Stoic idea inconsistent with the theology he intends to defend.

THE PROBLEM OF TERTULLIAN'S THEOLOGY

We are brought back, then, to our original problem: that of Tertullian's attitude toward the theology which he commends with such eloquence. There can be no doubt about his loyalty to the teaching of the Greek theology which he had inherited. He carefully reproduces the outlines of that Christianized Platonist world-view whose primitive form we have seen in Justin: the ingenerate God related to the generate world through the mediatorial offices of his Logos. But there is a puzzling quality about Tertullian's way of treating these themes. At times, as we have noted, he appears not to have understood it very well, not to have grasped its theoretical implications or presuppositions. And connected with this seeming lack of comprehension is another fact. It is not, so to speak, "from the inside" that Tertullian tries to work out the problems of this theology. His own thought is not so molded by this way of thinking that the questions which it raises are his own questions. On the contrary, he troubles himself only with problems which arise when some objector attacks one or another of its positions; and he is satisfied when he has offered a plausible defense of the views which he has inherited in the form in which he learned them.

And to these observations we may join another. Despite the differences between them, Justin and Irenaeus have in common one important characteristic, which they do not share with Tertullian. The religious ideal which is built into a Platonist world-picture is incorporated into their portrayal of the Christian life and its goal. If asked what was the nature of the good offered to men by Christ, both of them would have included in their answer a reference to the sharing of God's immortality through the knowledge of his Being. But this ideal, though native to the theology which he defends, plays little or no part in Tertullian's teaching. In other words, the natural religious "sense" of the doctrines which he expounds remains, for Tertullian, an insignificant part of their meaning; and this fact may well help to explain the puzzling way in which he appears to stand outside the system which he defends.

Taken together, these considerations cast no little light on Tertullian's attitude toward the Greek theology which he reproduces. He sees it, in effect, as involved in the Rule of Faith, which he is bound to defend against corruptors and detractors. When he enters the lists against Hermogenes or Marcion or Praxeas, he does so with only one primary motive: that of showing his opponents wrong and the tradition as he had received it right. His attention is engaged not by the theological problems for their own sake, but by the necessity for preserving unaltered the doctrinal basis of the life of the Christian community.

It would be easy, having said this much, to dismiss Tertullian as a somewhat imperceptive dogmatist. But to leave the matter there would be to risk a serious misunderstanding. If Tertullian is not directly interested in the sort of problem which is raised by the theology which he reproduces, this is because, for all his fidelity to the teaching of his predecessors, his own personal interest is engaged by problems of another form. It is not in the Greek search for the vision of a stable Reality that Tertullian finds his clue for understanding the meaning of man's life in the world. And, therefore, it is not in a theology of the Greek sort that he finds his key for explaining the thrust and significance of the Christian Gospel. What form, then, does the problem of God and the world assume in his mind?

GODS REAL AND UNREAL

An answer to this question involves an appreciation not of a theological system, but of a religious attitude. To ask it is to inquire what, in Tertullian's mind, are the *problems* to which the Christian revelation afforded a relevant answer. Hence, what we are trying to isolate is nothing so concrete as a doctrine. It is rather an outlook or perspective which is the more elusive for the fact that it is presupposed rather than formulated in plain language. What we must look for are clues to the mental posture which shapes Tertullian's sense of the significance of the Christian proclamation.

Our first clue can be found in one or two passages in which Tertullian suggests what, for him, is involved in faith and in the knowledge of God. In the first book of his work *Against Marcion,* Tertullian sets about combating the hypothesis of an "unknown God"—a God whom no man before the coming of Christ had either recognized or acknowledged. His attack takes the form of an argument that an unknown God cannot be a real God. To speak of an "unknown God," he insists, is to talk about a myth, a God who by hypothesis does nothing, and therefore cannot be real. The true God, on the other hand, is one whose reality is attested by the fact that his power and will are expressed in the fabrics of nature and history.[50] He is God precisely because he is in active control of what goes on in the world. If, Tertullian quips, Marcion's unknown God is to be believed, he "ought at least to have produced one stray vegetable as his own." [51] Otherwise, it is not clear what sense there is in calling him "God."

God, then, is one who cannot be absolutely unknown, for the very good reason that part of what is meant by calling him "God" is the fact that in his works he bears witness to the reality of his might. But Tertullian is not content merely to demand that God be knowable through the order of nature. The true God is also one who will make himself known by his direct teaching to man. Moreover, this teaching will have a different object than the appreciation of God's majesty through the beauties of the cosmic order. "On the ground of God's character, this too has been believed to be a divine function: to teach or to point out what is necessary in human affairs." [52] For Tertullian, the essential characteristic of the real God is the fact that the welfare and the destiny of man are in his hands. If, then, this God makes himself known, he will do so through his active intervention in, and concern for, the course of men's individual and collective lives. God is the Author of nature. But he is also the one who regulates and governs human existence in view of the end to which he wills to bring it. And as his activity extends itself to this sphere, so must his revelation, in the form of a teaching which makes known the pattern and meaning of human life.

Who, then, is the real God? He is the one to whom men may and must go to discover the sense of their own pilgrimage, and therewith the rules for its successful accomplishment. But conversely, for Tertullian, true religion is loyalty to the God who attests his power and his reality by making known the direction, the laws, and the goal of the life which man is presently leading. In Tertullian's eyes, this is the heart of the matter. Wisdom—as we have already heard him remark—consists in action which accords with the dispensation of God.[53] More fully expressed, this observation means two things: that the name "God" belongs properly to that supreme and active Will in whose counsels and decrees man's destiny is contained; and that man's calling is to give himself in obedience to this Will as it makes itself known.

GOD AND HISTORY

Something more of Tertullian's outlook is revealed incidentally in his discussions of the significance and validity of Old Testament prophecy. Since almost all that he says in this connection is taken over from Justin Martyr, the distinctive emphases in his presentation are fairly easy to detect. Justin had assumed, as does Tertullian, that the essential function of prophecy is prediction. He was therefore able to contend that the authority and inspiration of the Old Testament are established by the fulfillment of its prophecies in the life of Christ and the deeds of the apostolic community. Tertullian reproduces the form of this argument in a passage of his *Apology*. It requires to be quoted at length. Having already alluded to the antiquity of the Scriptures as one evidence of their authority, he continues:

> Now . . . we bring before you something of greater significance: the majesty of the Scriptures. . . . Nor need you wait long or look far to discover this. The things which will teach you are before your eyes: the world, the present age, the issues of events.
>
> Everything which happens was foretold; whatever we see was announced. The earth swallows up cities. The sea devours islands. Civil and foreign wars convulse the earth. Kingdoms collide with kingdoms. Territories are devastated by famine and by plague, by local disasters and by frequent death. The humble are exalted and the proud brought low. Justice grows rare; iniquity multiplies. Care for good habits of life declines. Even the seasons and the elements fail to fulfill their regular courses. The order of nature is disturbed by monstrous events and portents.
>
> Now all this was predicted and written down before it happened. While we suffer these evils we read about them. While we examine the Scriptures, they are verified.[54]

The logic of this argument, as we have said, is the same as that of Justin's. The divinity of the Scriptures is proved by their accurate prediction of events: "The truth of a prophecy (*divinatio*) is . . . a meet proof of its divine origin." [55]

But it is striking and significant that in this passage Tertullian lays all his emphasis on the fulfillment of Old Testament prophecy in public events of his own time. He portrays the Scriptures as the one satisfactory key for understanding the course of contemporary history. His attention is explicitly focused on "the world, the present age, the issues of events"; and the divinity of the Scriptures is seen in this: that their accuracy attests their source in the God who in fact controls and governs what comes to pass in the world of man's present experience. Tertullian evinces the same interest and the same attitude in another, and less studied, observation which he makes while describing the life of the Christian community. "We come together," he writes, "for the reading of the Holy Scriptures, whenever events of the present time compel us to seek either forewarnings of the future or interpretations of the past." [56] Again, the revelation in the Bible is valued for its immediate relevance to the course of history, its provision of a basis both for action and for understanding in the context of human affairs.

GOD AND THE GODS OF ROME

Both the importance of this appreciation of Scripture, and its relation to Tertullian's working definition of what is meant by "God," become clearer when they are viewed in the light of his formulation of the issue as between the Christian Church and the Roman Empire. He calls attention to the claim that the empire of Augustus and his successors has its foundation in the religious obedience with which Rome had conformed to the dictates of the divine powers which rule in human affairs. "I will not avoid," he writes, "the debate which arises out of the false allegation of those who say that it is as a reward for their zealous piety that the Romans have been raised to . . . such a height as to rule the world." [57] In this contention, Tertullian sees what is for him a crucial religious issue. In whose hands, as a matter of fact, does the destiny of mankind rest? To what source must a man go if he is to understand the course of human events? Latin thought had raised these questions and had sought an answer to them in the *religio* of the Roman State. Tertullian, a Latin himself, asks the same questions. But he finds a contrary answer.

It is of the essence of Tertullian's belief that the theology of the Roman State is a false one. He is willing and able to attack his opponents on the obvious issue of Roman "piety." He points out at elaborate length that the history of Rome is replete with acts of desecration and irreligion. This polemic, however, does not, as far as he is concerned, go to the heart of the matter. More important to him is the traditional Christian argument that the gods of Rome are unreal, and that a piety which has them as its object is therefore meaningless. He does not, to be sure, deny them all existence. Like his predecessors, he is willing to concede them the status of demons whose object is the ruin of mankind. It is a part of the malice and subtlety of these beings, he says, that they use their acquaintance with scriptural prophecy to simulate an independent knowledge of the future, and a control over human destiny, and thus make themselves out to be gods. But their claim is a fraud; and this fact is attested by their fear and their powerlessness both before Christ and before believers who have the Spirit of Christ.

In vain, then, do the gods of Rome arrogate to themselves a majesty and a might which they do not possess. It is not in their declarations that the secrets of human destiny are to be found, nor by their will that the "issues of events" are controlled. The truth is found in the Christian Scriptures; and the true God is the one whom those Scriptures make known. "There is no other God than the one to whom we belong," [58] says Tertullian.

See, then, if the dispenser of kingdoms is not that One who is master both of the world which is ruled and of the man who rules it. See if the One who controls the rise and fall of empires, and assigns to each its time in the present age, is not the One who was before all time and made the present age a sum of eras. See if the One who causes states to rise and fall is not the One who ruled over the human race when there were no states.[59]

That is, Tertullian persists, see if the ruler of the destiny of Rome is not in fact the God of the Jews, the Lord whom the Scriptures proclaim and to whom Christians pray for the welfare of the emperor.

GOD AND WORLD IN TERTULLIAN

In his argument against Marcion, then, in his assertion of the "majesty" of the Scriptures, and in his polemic against Roman religion, Tertullian displays a common interest and outlook. In each of these connections, his mind is occupied with a uniform set of themes. He is in search of the true God. But this, as it turns out, does not mean, for him, the God who lies at the end of an intellectual quest for stable Reality. It means, rather, the God whose reality consists in his being the ultimate arbiter and governor of the "issues of events," of the public course of human affairs. Consequently, when Tertullian turns to the Scriptures, he looks to them for a revelation of what God has done, is doing, and will do in the world. In Tertullian's eyes, this is exactly what the Christian dispensation makes fully and finally manifest. It publishes for all to understand an account of what the Creator is up to in his creation. It calls attention to certain events and persons in or through whom God has directly declared or effected his will. It explains the end to which God is bringing the world—the imminent "last things," resurrection, judgment, hell, and heaven. Finally, it sets forth a pattern of belief and life which, if it is followed, will bring the life of mankind into accord with the divine purpose which is the hidden sense of history.

Given this pattern of religious interest, it is not difficult to see why Tertullian's mind is not wholly captive to the theological world-picture of Greek Christian thought. His outlook is in many respects typically Latin—or better, perhaps, Roman. His attention is focused on the concrete flow of events in human history. He sees this history as undergirded and determined by a Power which is more than human, and whose purposes are manifested in certain portentous events and oracular teachings. In accordance with this attitude, Tertullian understands piety to consist in a sensitive obedience to the divine Will which is thus made known. For him, therefore, the world is in the first instance the sphere of human action and responsibility. It is an arena of decisions—decisions, however, whose meaning can only be estimated in the light of the precedents out of which they arise and the consequences to which they lead. The adequate human life, collective or individual, is one whose decisions constitute a pattern of obedience to past events in which the divine purpose has been revealed, and thus lead on toward a final conformity with the goal which that purpose seeks. Tertullian knows of the world as a *kosmos,* a natural order; and like every educated Latin, he takes this Greek world seriously. But the world in which he lives mentally is a framework of decision and action, ordered primarily not in space, whether physical or metaphysical, but in time. Except secondarily, the subject of his religious interest is not the unchanging structure of things, but the changing flow of event and action which leads to divine judgment in the end, as it flows from divine creation in the beginning.

Conceived in this way, the world is evaluated from a perspective which is alien to Greek habits of thought. Despite his dutiful use of Justin's philosophical terminology, Tertullian does not in practice understand the world as "generate," or finite. Certainly, he makes little or no use of Irenaeus's notion that salvation history can be pictured as the "dispensation" by which God elevates mankind from generate existence to a sharing in immortal life. As he views it, the created order is a span of time whose meaning emerges in a conflict between the purpose of God and the purposes of rebellious creaturely wills. The resolution of this conflict is at hand. That is the significance of the coming of Christ, whose work presages the final victory of God's will, and whose present power is revealed in the Christian's freedom to do God's will. But the conflict continues, and the world remains alienated from God, since its final manifestation as the obedient instrument of his purpose awaits a future dispensation and a new age.

Therefore, as Tertullian sees it, the Christian life is necessarily a rigorous struggle: an act of ever-renewed and costly obedience to God in the midst of an age in which God's sovereignty is actively denied and opposed. The future belongs to the Christians because it is they who preserve in their belief and in their lives the truth which the future will validate. But in the present age, in a world under the immediate power of rebellious spirits, they represent an opposition—beleaguered, tempted, and oppressed—who laugh only when the world weeps, and weep when the world laughs. Their calling is to live within the world as men who, by patterning their decisions and actions on God's past revelation of himself, claim for themselves the future which he, the true Ruler of the world, is bringing to pass through his Word.

CONCLUSION

It is in the light of this outlook that one must evaluate Tertullian's attitude toward the Rule of Faith and his use of the rational theology of the Greek-Christian tradition. The Rule of Faith, as a doctrinal summary of God's past revelation of himself, is an essential part of that truth which is the Christian's key to the future. Fidelity to it in the present constitutes the identity of the community which will inherit God's promises for the age to come. For just this reason, Tertullian is uncompromising in his insistence that the Rule must be maintained in a whole and uncorrupted form; and his interest in the problems of ra-

tional theology stems from his recognition that these problems
are involved in the assertion of his faith that the God of the
Scriptures is the one ultimate Ruler of the course of human affairs. Such sectarians as Marcion and Hermogenes are, therefore,
doubly guilty from Tertullian's point of view. They are guilty
in the first place of seeking to alter the clear sense of the tradition which the Christian community guards as the mark of its
identity and the basis of its hope. But they are guilty also of un-
dermining what is both a part of that tradition and the essential
presupposition of its content: the teaching that God the Creator
is the absolute Sovereign who by his Word makes, sustains, and
redeems the world. Tertullian sees, on the contrary, in the theology of the Greek Christian tradition, a defense and assertion
of this teaching. Therefore, he uses this theology and, in his own
way, develops it.

Yet to him—and here we return to our original observation
—this theology is important because he understands it to say
what the Rule of Faith contains. He has little appreciation or
concern for its larger philosophical or religious implications. This
is no doubt the explanation of his apparent lack of interest, as we
have perhaps unjustly called it, in the problems of rational theology. He does not lack interest in them. But his interest is limited to their bearing upon the apostolic tradition as he understands it; and the coherence which he looks for in his theology
is its coherence with the Rule of Faith, not its systematic intellectual coherence as a speculative creation.

And in any case, as we have seen, Tertullian's world-picture, his way of thinking about God and the world, is built on
another basis than that of the Christianized Platonism which he
inherited. It is in fact determined by the reception of Christian
teaching into a Latin or Roman world-view, whose distinguishing characteristic is its interest in the world as a course of events
informed by divine Purpose. For one who shares this outlook,
the rational theology of the Greeks, with its idea of the world
as *kosmos,* is a subsidiary, though fascinating and necessary, sup-

plement. Through Tertullian, the Latin Church inherited the theology of Greek Christianity translated into its own idiom. But like Tertullian himself, it accepted this theology more as a *datum* than as a focus of continuing creative interest. Its own attention was naturally concentrated upon the problems of Christian obedience, in this world, to that divine revelation which is man's key to a future blessedness.

Notes to Chapter IV

1. *Res.* 3.1.
2. *Praescr.* 36.5.
3. See p. 83.
4. *Marc.* I.1.6.
5. *Praescr.* 37.1.
6. *Marc.* I.19.2 f.
7. *Praescr.* 14.4.
8. *Praescr.* 9.3 f.
9. *Praescr.* 7.8, cf. Col. 2.8.
10. *Herm.* 8.2.
11. *Praescr.* 30.1.
12. *Praescr.* 7.3.
13. *Res.* 3.6.
14. *Praescr.* 7.9 ff.
15. *Res.* 3.2.
16. *Ap.* 47.1 f., cf. *Carn.* 9.2.
17. Cf. *Ap.* 11.5.
18. *Ap.* 17.4–5; but see esp. the treatise *De testimonio animae.*
19. *Res.* 3.1; and see pp. 51 f.
20. *Ap.* 17.6.
21. *Praescr.* 36.4.
22. *Praescr.* 13.1 ff.
23. *Prax.* 2.
24. *Herm.* 1.3.
25. *Herm.* 2.1.
26. *Ap.* 17.1.
27. Gen. 1.1.
28. *Herm.* 20.3.
29. *Herm.* 33.1.
30. *Herm.* 4.5.
31. Cf. *Herm.* 4.1, 6.1; *Marc.* I.8.9.
32. *Ap.* 17.2.
33. *Marc.* I.4.2.
34. *Ibid.*
35. *Marc.* I.8.2.
36. *Carn.* 3.4 f.
37. *Marc.* I.25.3.
38. *Marc.* I.11.3.
39. Cf. *Prax.* 7, 8.
40. *Herm.* 18.3.
41. *Herm.* 18.1.
42. *Ap.* 48.7, 11.
43. *Ap.* 21.10.
44. *Res.* 5.6.
45. *Prax.* 14.3.
46. *Herm.* 18.2.
47. *Prax.* 5.
48. *Prax.* 9.2.
49. *Prax.* 8.5.
50. Cf. *Marc.* I.18.2.
51. *Marc.* I.11.5.
52. *Ibid.*
53. See pp. 101 f.
54. *Ap.* 20.1 ff.
55. *Ap.* 20.3.
56. *Ap.* 39.3.
57. *Ap.* 25.2.
58. *Ap.* 24.1.
59. *Ap.* 26.1.

CHAPTER V. *Origen – A New Christian Platonism*

In the work of Justin and Irenaeus, we have seen the beginnings of the process by which the early Church developed a rational or philosophical account of the world in its relation with God. Stimulated by the necessities of apologetic and by the demands of their polemic against Gnosticism, such Christian thinkers drew, consciously or unconsciously, on the resources of Greek theology in order to evolve a coherent statement of the philosophical implications of Christian teaching. The fruit of their efforts was not a finished product, but a tentative scheme whose structure rested on certain fundamental ideas: the uniquely ingenerate Creator; the Logos-Son; the generate character of the created order. Tertullian, in the West, employed and defended these conceptions in his attacks on sectarian teaching. They were for him a part of the Rule of Faith. But his personal religious understanding of the world and of God was shaped in another mold than that of the Greek theology which he reproduced. We must therefore look elsewhere than to Tertullian for a constructive revision and restatement of the preliminary theological essays of the apologists and Irenaeus.

We must look, in fact, away from the West altogether and turn to the Egyptian metropolis of Alexandria. There, at the beginning of the third century, there appeared a theologian whose work was to influence the shape of Christian thought for centuries to come: Origen. Born around A.D. 186, Origen taught both in Alexandria itself and in Palestine, where he died at the age of sixty-eight or sixty-nine, as the result of a term of imprisonment for his faith. His whole life was taken up with intellectual pursuits. An apologist in his own right, he was nevertheless in the first instance a student of the Christian Scriptures, to whose interpretation he brought the resources of a mind trained in the methods of Greek literary criticism as well as in philosophy.

Through his students, and through his voluminous writings, Origen transmitted a teaching which contained the germs of innumerable later developments in the life and thought of the Church. Much studied, attacked, and defended, Origen was something of a theological storm center even before his death, and he has remained so to this day. He has been variously presented as the betrayer of Christianity to Platonism; the founder of biblical theology; the inventor of Arianism; the father of Trinitarian orthodoxy; the forerunner of Christian monasticism; the betrayer of the biblical ethic. There is, one suspects, at least a grain of truth in all these allegations, but then, Origen's was a complex mind. And though his posterity at one point renounced him as a heretic, it did not forget the lessons which he had taught it. He remains a man whose thought has stimulated and instructed every generation which has sought to understand it. With Origen, in more senses than one, Christian theology came suddenly of age.

But it came of age in a form which reflected Origen's distinctive intellectual and religious background. Much of Origen's greatness—and more than a little of the bafflement and irritation which he inspires in his interpreters—has its root in the unstudied ease with which he blends together the Christian faith which he learned from his parents and the philosophical outlook which he took over from the Christian and non-Christian intellectuals of his cosmopolitan native city. In his thought, these two elements are so wedded as to be indeed one flesh. Origen is the continual despair of those who try to impugn his Christianity by pointing to his Platonism, or to minimize his philosophical leanings by calling attention to the scriptural and ecclesiastical elements in his thought. In Origen, Christian faith and philosophical understanding are no longer exterior to each other—as they are even in such a writer as Justin Martyr; and this remains true in principle even though his thought reflects the tensions and ambiguities which arise from his effort to express this unified vision. His teaching has a remarkable integrity of spirit, which stems from the fact that he was, as a man, a representative product of his whole environment: an expositor of Christian teaching who was at the same time a serious and constructively interested student of Greek thought.

ORIGEN'S BACKGROUND

What, then, were the sources and stimuli of Origen's thought? And what were the methods and presuppositions with which he approached the problems of rational theology?

Origen had predecessors and teachers, and their work he both continued and severely criticized. Among these we must, needless to say, include the Greek apologists and Irenaeus. Much of what Origen says can be understood as an attempt to produce a more coherent and self-consistent version of the teaching put forward by these, and other, Christian writers of an earlier generation.

But the more immediate influences on Origen's thought must be looked for in the intellectual culture of Alexandria itself, where pagan, Jewish, Christian, and Gnostic teachers rubbed shoulders, exchanged ideas, and debated their respective positions. Origen learned not a little, positively as well as negatively, from Gnostic divines, from the writings of Philo of Alexandria, as well as from the thought of one who may have been his own master (though Origen never mentions him): Clement of Alexandria. From men of this sort, he took over his general approach to the problems of exegesis and theology, as also the range of questions and issues which for him made up the subject matter of theological reflection. By the same token, he shared with these thinkers a common philosophical idiom, that of later Platonism, with its varying admixtures of Stoic, Aristotelian, and Pythagorean ideas.

The influence of this environment on Origen's outlook becomes obvious when we note two instructive differences between him and his Latin counterpart, Tertullian. One of these differences relates to the character of their learning. Tertullian was by no means a poorly read man. But whatever may have been the scope of his reading, he was in no real sense a "student" of Greek philosophy. The opposite was true of Origen. When Origen talked philosophy, he knew, and cared, what he was saying. There are external testimonies to his erudition. The Church historian Eusebius makes a great point of it, as does Origen's pupil, Gregory Thaumaturgus, in his *Panegyric*. But the best evidence is provided by Origen himself in his own writings, and especially perhaps in the book *Against Celsus*, which reveals the extent and detail of his acquaintance with both the Stoic and Platonic traditions. Whatever Origen thought of the value of Greek philosophy, there can be no doubt that unlike most of his Christian predecessors, he was at least as well acquainted with it as the better pagan teachers of his time.

And if Origen was a master of the intellectual tradition which lay behind the eclectic Platonism of his time, he was also indebted to it for his understanding of the nature of the religious problem. For Tertullian, we have seen, the central religious issue was that of the obedience of the will to the truth which God has made known and the way of life which he has commanded. By active loyalty to divine revelation, man allies himself to that sovereign Purpose which controls the future, and which promises eternal life to those who accept its grace and its demand as they are made known in Christ. This conception of the nature and significance of the Christian life issues in a preoccupation with the moral and doctrinal purity of the Church and its members, and returns over and again to the fundamental problem of the will and its adhesion to God. To Origen, however, such an outlook is alien. What absorbs him is the problem of the soul's attainment of that contemplative knowledge which perfects it in the likeness of God. As he sees it, the soul is made to share in the incorruptible life of God, and Christian revelation is the divinely provided means by which it can realize this destiny. Origen thus concentrates on the same issues which had engaged the interest of Plato and his later disciples: the nature of the soul, and the way by which it returns, through knowledge, to unity with its divine Source. In treating of Christianity as a way of salvation, Origen therefore emphasizes the growth of the soul in spiritual understanding—in that interior grasp of divine mysteries by which it is transformed into the image of the Truth which it apprehends. However much Origen may differ from the Platonism of the pagan schools—and his teaching in fact diverges from it widely at certain crucial points—there can be no doubt that his conception of the point and purpose of Christian teaching is shaped by the Platonist idea of the soul's intellectual quest for union with intelligible Reality.

THE CENTRALITY OF REVELATION

Having said this, however, it becomes immediately important to notice that there is one basic way in which Origen recasts the whole logic of Platonism. Like every Christian teacher, Origen firmly believes that the possibility of the soul's spiritual progress depends upon God's revelation of himself, and not upon the unaided capacity of the soul to "discover" God. The revealed character of the knowledge of God is thus a first principle with Origen; and it determines both his estimate of the achievements of Greek thought, and his account of the means by which the Christian is brought to the realized likeness of God.

It is probably not necessary to say a great deal here about Origen's views on the status and accomplishments of Greek philosophy: not because they are without intrinsic interest, but because in all essentials they reproduce the attitude which we have already met in earlier Christian thinkers. Like Justin, Origen acknowledges certain correspondences between Christian teaching and that of the philosophers. He records his agreement with Plato on certain issues, for example, and his admiration for the ethics of the Stoa. Moreover, he accounts for these coincidences of doctrine by use of the same hypotheses which we have found in Justin, Irenaeus, and even Tertullian. Origen asserts repeatedly that the teachings of the philosophers are anticipated by Moses, the prophets, and Solomon; and he adduces this fact as evidence that in certain cases the former have borrowed from the latter. For a yet more general explanation of these agreements, he points to the natural knowledge both of God and of the principles of morality which is implanted in every man, and which he seems to regard as a primitive and universal revelation. Origen therefore concurs with St. Paul that no man has been left without some knowledge of God.

But the conclusion which Origen infers from this truth is by no means complimentary to the achievements of Greek philosophy. By reason both of the character and of the spirit of its teaching, he thinks, it has corrupted the knowledge which was granted to it. It has failed, for one thing, in the practical task of making the knowledge of God available to ordinary people and thus confirming them in that virtuous life which it is the business of the philosopher to practice and to inculcate. Greek wisdom, whatever truth it may possess, has no power to convert souls, and no meaning for any save an intellectual elite. Moreover, the philosopher's pride in his own intellectual accomplishments renders him impervious to the teaching of God. He sets up his own vision as the final truth, and in this way becomes an idolater, perverting the knowledge which has been granted him by refusing attentive obedience to the Giver of all knowledge. Origen's strictures on philosophy are no less severe and no less emphatic than those brought by other authors whom we have surveyed—though he lacks both the indifference of an Irenaeus, and the exaggerated bitterness of a Tertullian.

Origen sums up the situation as he sees it in his late treatise *Against Celsus:*[1]

> If . . . God really had been found by Plato or one of the Greeks, they would not have reverenced anything else and called it God and worshiped it, either abandoning the true God or combining with the majesty of God things which ought not to be associated with Him. But we affirm that human nature is not sufficient in any way to seek for God and to find Him in His pure nature, unless it is helped by the God who is the object of the search. And he is found by those who, after doing what they can, admit that they need Him. . . .

The true knowledge of God is the product not of speculation, but of obedient waiting on God's own Word. Therefore, one cannot expect to find such knowledge among those whose sole reliance is their own insight.

It may seem remarkable that a Christian thinker who is himself so obviously a disciple of Greek thought should take so dim a view of its achievements. But Origen's position is not so paradoxical as may at first glance appear. His attacks on Greek philosophy are aimed specifically at its religious insufficiencies, at its failure to attain and disseminate a true knowledge of God. Such knowledge, he argues, can only be found in Christian revelation, where it is given in a form which makes it available to all men, and not solely to the talented and the enlightened. This contention, however, does not involve Origen in a negative judgment either on the aims of philosophy (which he shares), or on its ordinary stock of basic religious and ethical ideas (which he accepts as commonplaces, familiar to all). In the light of Christian revelation, one can perceive the errors and limitations of the philosophers; and one can acknowledge that their speculations are not to be trusted in detail. But the framework of philosophical understanding, the presuppositions and rational methods which the philosopher employs, is not invalidated by such criticism. On the contrary, it can stand—but now as a tool for understanding and articulating God's revelation of himself in the Scriptures. Origen's pupils, we gather, were made to study philosophy to just this end: not in order that they might accept the conclusions of some one school of thought, but in order that the disciplines and axioms of philosophical reflection might fit them to grasp and defend the intellectual content of Christian revelation, itself the true philosophy.

In its positive role, then, philosophy is a tool. But the substance of truth, for Origen, is found in the Scriptures. On this point both his stated views and his theological practice are clear and coherent. "We . . . ," he explains, "believe that there is no possible way . . . of bringing to man's knowledge the higher and diviner teaching about the Son of God, except by means of those scriptures which were inspired by the Holy Spirit, namely, the gospels, and the writings of the apostles, to which we add, according to the declaration of Christ himself, the law and the prophets." [2] And Origen shaped the pattern of his own activities and employments to accord with this principle. The one work to which he dedicated himself was the interpretation of the inspired books; the establishment of their text, and the careful exposition of its meaning. To this task, he brought all the resources which lay to his hand: the techniques of textual and literary criticism, first of all, but also the methods of philosophical analysis and deduction.

It is at this point that we can begin to appreciate the tendency of Origen's position. He reaffirms the traditional Christian view that saving knowledge of God is the product of God's self-revelation. Moreover, he associates this revelation exclusively with the literature of the Bible, which he treats as an inspired text. But he does not, for this reason, suppose that there is no place in Christianity for the rational investigation of truth. The anti-intellectualism and "fundamentalism" of Tertullian would have found no very sympathetic reception with him. For Origen agrees with Plato that man's final blessedness lies in the fulfillment of his vocation to *know*, "to nourish the soul and enlighten the mind with the food of truth and wisdom." [3] Where he differs with Plato is in his estimate of the method by which such knowledge is to be attained. The education which Plato gave to his students was intended to lead them, through the discipline of mathematics, to an appreciation of the harmonies of the cosmic order, and then beyond, to a grasp of the immaterial truth which is the foundation of cosmic order. But Origen proposes a quite different kind of education. His students are led not to contemplate the heavens, but to study the Scriptures; and the dialectical method which they use is not aimed at the construction of a theological physics, but at the comprehension of the mysteries which God has hidden in the inspired words of the Bible. Origen thus reconstructs and refocuses the Platonic ideal of the lover of wisdom. He seeks the wisdom which God gives, and he seeks it at the hands of God, in the Bible. But at the same time the goal of his enterprise remains much the same as that of Plato's: the progress of the soul, through rational activity, to fellowship with the Divine.

Thus, the analogy between Origen's outlook and that of classical Platonism extends to his understanding of the role of the Bible in the Christian life. The Alexandrian teacher held that there is a form of intellectual occupation which is an intrinsic part of the believer's vocation, and not merely an occasional or peripheral activity undertaken for apologetic or polemical motives. This enterprise, which is thus an essential ingredient in the religious discipline by which the soul is brought to perfection, is the purposeful and exacting study of the Scriptures. It employs a rational method, under the guidance and inspiration of the Holy Spirit. And its product is *theology* in the proper sense of that term: an interior grasp of the mysteries of divine Wisdom, and thus communion with God himself.

But this assessment of the role of the Bible is further connected in Origen's mind with his understanding of its character as an inspired book. It presupposes that the Scriptures in fact require to be studied as well as read—that their meaning, although plain enough at one level, is in other respects obscure and hidden.

Of course, this was no new idea. Christians before the time of Origen had insisted that the meaning of the Jewish Law and Prophets must remain obscure unless they were understood as foreshadowing and announcing Christ; and there is every indication that they also found certain recorded teachings of the Lord and his Apostles hard to interpret. But when Origen speaks of the obscurity of Scripture, of its containing "mysteries," he means something rather different than just the fact that the Old Testament can only be understood retrospectively, in terms of its fulfillment, or that certain passages in the Bible are difficult to understand. He means that the inspired books are not always explicit in making known the things of God. Even the man who has managed to grasp clearly the literal sense of a given sentence or paragraph cannot be sure that he has laid hold on the full meaning of the text. Quite often, no doubt, this is because the Scriptures state their teaching without making plain either its presuppositions or its implications; and in such cases, full understanding is achieved only by comparing different passages and by using the techniques of logical analysis to draw out the truths which are hidden there.

But this is not all. From his predecessors and contemporaries in Alexandria—from Philo, from Clement, and from the exegetical procedures of Gnostic teachers—Origen had learned that the highest truth in the inspired text can only be appropriated by one who goes beyond the literal to the "spiritual" or symbolic meaning of what is written. He explains that since "the scriptures were composed through the Spirit of God . . . they have not only that meaning which is obvious, but also another which is hidden from the majority of readers. For the contents of scripture are the outward forms of certain mysteries and the images of divine things." [4] In other words, the plain sense of what the Bible says is meaningful in two ways: in itself, and as an intimation or symbol of higher truths. It is in this way that Origen's Platonism extends to his conception of the character of the Scriptures themselves. He believes that the Bible has an inner meaning which is only partially reflected in its outward and literal sense. Just as Plato had seen in the harmonious motions of the visible world an intimation and an image of the intelligible order which was their stable counterpart, so Origen sees in the explicit teaching of the Bible truths which are at the same time reflections of an implicit higher truth—"images of divine things." And the task of the exegete, as he sees it, is by investigation, under the guidance of God's Spirit, to come to a knowledge of this "spiritual" wisdom.

THE GENESIS OF ORIGEN'S WORLD-PICTURE

It is in the light of this understanding of the assumptions, goals, and methods of Christian theology that we must approach the question of Origen's religious world-picture. The wisdom which Origen seeks and finds in the Scriptures is concerned in the first instance with the mysteries of redemption: with the relation of the soul to God in Christ, with the conditions and forms of its interior enlightenment, with the stages on its way to likeness with God. But a grasp of the deep truths of human redemption implies and involves something more. It presupposes a theory about the nature of man, his relation to God, and the character of the finite world of which he is a part. These problems, too, find their corresponding answers in the revelation of God; and it is a natural part of the work of a theologian to show what these answers are—to delineate the world-picture which is conveyed (whether directly, or by implication, or symbolically) in the words of the Bible.

The basic outlines of this world-picture were, of course, well known. They were a part of the explicit teaching of the Scriptures, and they had already been formulated in certain of the axioms of the Church's Rule of Faith. This Origen acknowledged. Like Tertullian, he was conscious of being the heir of a tradition which set out the elementary presuppositions of biblical theology as earlier Christian generations had worked them out. And also like Tertullian, Origen accepted this tradition as authoritative. But he differed from his western contemporary in two important ways. He did not think that the Rule as he knew it had said everything which could be known or which ought to be known. And furthermore, he thought that there were significant questions and problems which the traditional theology summarized in the Rule had failed to meet. In Origen's mind, therefore, the biblical interpreter had a job to do which was more than merely defensive. It was his business to seek a fuller understanding of the doctrine whose elements were already specified in the tradition, and by this means to exhibit the true proportions of Christian teaching about man, the world, and God.

What this means in plain language is that Origen's reflections on theological problems had led him to reconsider and reinterpret the teaching which he had inherited from such writers as Justin and Irenaeus. This teaching already reflected the incorporation into Christian thought of ideas drawn from the Greek philosophical tradition. But from the perspective of his own relatively more exact understanding of the prevalent Platonist philosophy, Origen was bound to be critical of the work of his predecessors. This, needless to say, was not because they had made use of philosophical conceptions in their exposition of Christian doctrine. Rather, it was because they had done so without a full awareness of the implications of the language which they employed. From the point of view of the philosophical outlook which they had themselves exploited, their teaching was not fully coherent. It is for this reason that Origen offers his reinterpretation, which is intended not as a repudiation of the tradition, but as an explanation and development of its meaning.

THE BASIC PROBLEM

We can get some notion of the source of Origen's dissatisfaction by attending to his formulation of a general principle which underlies all his teaching. He bases his exposition of this principle on the words of St. Paul in II Corinthians 4:18, "The things that are seen are temporal, but the things which are not seen are eternal." On this Origen comments:

> To those who can understand . . . [St. Paul] obviously means the sensible world, though he calls it 'the things that are seen', and the intelligible world which is comprehensible by the mind alone, though he calls it 'the things that are not seen'. He also knows that sensible things are temporal and visible, while intelligible things are eternal and invisible.[5]

In other words, the Apostle agrees with Plato in distinguishing two kinds of existence, Being and Becoming. Origen insists, moreover, that this picture of the world is a governing presupposition of the Christian way of life. Indeed, he argues that in their belief and conduct alike, Christians take it more seriously to heart than do the disciples of Plato. With the followers of Christ, he says,

> It is not merely a matter of theory when they distinguish between being and becoming and between what is intelligible and what is visible, and when they associate truth with being and by all possible means avoid the error that is bound up with becoming. They look, as they have learnt, not at the things which are becoming, which are seen and on that account temporal, but at the higher things, whether one wishes to call them 'being', or things 'invisible' because they are intelligible, or 'things which are not seen' because their nature lies outside the realm of sense-perception.[6]

Here Origen reveals the practical foundation of his theology: a distinctively Platonist foundation, which, however, he justifies not by appealing to Plato, but by quoting St. Paul. There is a "lower" and a "higher" kind of existence. The one is involved in time, change, and error; the other is the motionless and timeless realm of truth. The one is the visible, material world; the other, the invisible and spiritual world. All this is familiar enough. But we must note two facts. The first is that Origen uses this conception, not casually, but deliberately and with a full understanding of its implications. The second is that he does not use it in the first instance as a convenient device for explaining the difference between God and the finite order. He sees in it the key for understanding man's situation and his vocation as rational spirit. Man's happiness, the realization of his natural character, consists in communion with Being; and the attainment of this goal involves a turning away, a repudiation, of bodily or material existence. So much at any rate Origen is prepared to assume as fundamental.

But these affirmations immediately raise problems—and rather basic ones—from the point of view of traditional Christian teaching. They are not, in principle, new problems. Origen's Christian predecessors had made use of Platonist language of this sort, and the difficulties which he faces were implicit in their doctrine. But it is typical of Origen that he sees these problems clearly and tries to solve them rationally.

First of all, there is the question of the status of the human soul. Plato had explained the soul's affinity for Being, its vocation to share in ingenerate life, simply by arguing that it is itself eternal and spiritual by *nature*. Christian writers had gladly adopted the idea that the soul is called to participate in a divine mode of existence. It appealed to them as a convenient way of interpreting one aspect of the Christian eschatological hope. But at the same time, they had denied the logical basis of this belief by insisting that soul, like body, is *generate*. For how can a "creature" be naturally akin to changeless and undying Being? This is one question to which Origen will have to give some sort of answer.

But it is only one—and not even the most obvious or pressing. For the Platonist principle which Origen accepts seems further to imply that there is some intrinsic defect in the material world, something "wrong" with physical and visible existence. And Origen is not only aware of this implication, he believes that the Scriptures support it. "Our wise men," he writes, "speak disparagingly of all sensible nature, so that in one place our bodies are said to be 'futility' in the words: 'For the creation was made subject to futility, not of its own choice, but because of him who subjected it in hope.' " [7] Material, visible existence, as Origen understands it, is what makes for multiplicity, inequality, and diversity in the world. It is by nature far removed from the unity, harmony, and equality which characterize the spiritual order. And for just this reason, it is to some degree the contrary of the good.

But how well does this view consist with the doctrine that the world is the creation of the omnipotent goodness of God? Does Origen mean that matter is a principle of disorder independent of God, so as to deny divine omnipotence? Or does he mean that God is responsible for the creation of evil, so as to deny divine goodness? And does he not in either case call in question the truth which Irenaeus had been at such pains to assert—the truth that the physical component of man's nature is itself framed to receive the qualities of ingenerate existence? What does Origen believe about "matter," and what is his account of the problem of evil?

ORIGEN'S THEODICY

In his youthful treatise *On First Principles,* Origen offers a solution of these problems which he thinks is philosophically credible, scriptural in character, and directly contrary to the dualism of the Gnostics. His solution is based on two principles, the first of which he states directly: "God the Creator of the universe is both good and just and omnipotent. Now when 'in the beginning' he created what he wished to create . . . , he had no other reason for creating them except himself, that is, his goodness." [8] These words are a reaffirmation of the content of the tradition. The one God is the sole Author of all that is, and made all things "when before they did not exist." Furthermore, all the work of God is expressive of his goodness.

Consequently, Origen insists, as he must, that evil is not a matter of "nature." It is neither a principle independent of God, nor a creation of God. Evil—and here again he reiterates the traditional Christian teaching—is an affair of the *will*. "In our view," he writes, "it is not true that 'the matter which dwells among mortals' is responsible for evils. Each person's mind is responsible for the evil which exists in him, and this is what evil is. Evils are the actions which result from it. *In our view nothing else is strictly speaking evil*," [9] including matter itself. Thus, it is through the decisions of unconstrained creaturely wills, and not as a result of their embodiment or involvement in materiality, that evil exists in the world.

But do these explanations really serve the purpose for which they are intended? Origen thinks that in principle they do. Nevertheless, he sees that they are incomplete. For one thing, they do not explain how, if an appeal to the fact of embodiment is ruled out, it is possible for a rational spirit to go wrong, to act irrationally. For another, they fail to account for the fact—which experience, Scripture, and the wisdom of the philosophers agree in acknowledging—that matter, the principle of Becoming, does represent a factor of disharmony and irrationality in the world, even if it is not "strictly speaking evil." For Origen's position to be coherent, therefore, he must still deal with the two problems of the nature of the soul and the status of matter.

CREATION AND FALL

In undertaking this task, however, he adheres firmly to his initial stand. He insists that the state of the world as it is must be accounted for strictly in terms of the two factors he has specified: the omnipotent power of God, and the free initiative of rational spirits. And to explain how this can be so, he expounds his remarkable theory of the origin of the world. Since God, he writes, "in whom was neither variation, nor change, nor lack of power, was the cause of all things created, he created all his creatures equal and alike, for the simple reason that there was in him no cause that could give rise to variety and diversity." [10] God's original creation, then, was not a world of inequality and diversity, but a world of perfect rational harmony, in which all things shared a common nature and a common perfection. And since, as it goes without saying, these original creatures were as like as possible to God himself, they were rational spirits, capable of knowing and enjoying God. It was, therefore, upon the action of these creaturely minds that the future state of the world depended.

But these spirits were not only rational and equal. They were also free, and therefore able to become other than what God had made them to be. Origen explains why this is necessarily so: "since these rational beings, which as we said above were made in the beginning, were made when before they did not exist, by this very fact that they did not exist and then began to exist, they are of necessity subject to change and alteration." [11] Here Origen makes use of an idea which Irenaeus had already employed for much the same purpose. The capacity of rational spirits to go wrong does not depend upon their involvement in materiality. It stems from the fact that there is a certain quality of instability and imperfection which naturally attaches to beings whose existence is derivative. The souls which God originally created are morally changeable, for the reason that "whatever may have been the goodness that existed in their being, it existed in them not by nature but as a result of their Creator's benefi-cence." [12] In other words, it is the nature of any generate being to move and to change. But when such a being is also *rational*, the direction of its motions is determined by its own state of mind. Thus, Origen writes, "The Creator granted to the minds created by him the power of free and voluntary movement, in order that the good that was in them might become their own as being preserved by their own free will." [13]

In fact, however, God's purpose for his creatures was not realized. Their innate tendency to move and to alter took them not closer to God, but away from him: "sloth and weariness of taking trouble to preserve the good, coupled with disregard and neglect of better things, began the process of withdrawal from the good." [14] It is interesting that even at this point Origen can-not bring himself to attribute evil to the initiative of the rational souls. He is too good a Christian to attribute the fall of man to the passions and distractions which result from embodiment. But he is too good a Platonist to believe that a rational spirit can deliberately and knowingly rebel against the Good. Conse-quently, he appeals to the limitations of finitude—to change-ability, or sloth, or weariness—to explain the fact of sin. To admit more than this would be to deny the basis of his whole doctrine of man: the idea that the natural tendency of the ra-tional spirit is to seek its good in the contemplation and enjoy-ment of Being. He speaks of creaturely "freedom" as the root of evil; but what he means in practice by "freedom" is change-ability combined with a limited capacity for the appreciation of goodness.

But what is the *result* of the fall of the rational spirits? It is, in a word, the *diversification* of the created order. Origen explains that not all the rational creatures withdrew from God to the same degree: there were differences among them in re-spect to the depth of their fall. And it is from this fact that the present diversity and variety of the world stems. "From this source, it appears, the Creator of all things obtained certain seeds and causes of variety and diversity, in order that, according to the diversity of minds, that is, of rational beings, . . . he might create a world which was various and diverse." [15] Thus, the inequalities and disharmonies of the world-order in its present state are the result of sin; and its variegated structure reflects exactly the merits of the several spirits whose home it is.

And this, of course, is the point at which *matter* appears. For, as Origen observes, "the diversity of the world cannot exist apart from bodies." [16] Matter is the principle of distention, the expression of multiplicity and differentiation. Consequently, the appearance of differences among the rational spirits—differences which mark the varying degrees of their fall—is coincident with the appearance of the physical world, God's second-best creation. In itself, this visible world is not evil. Rather, in Origen's eyes, it is at once a symptom of evil, and a demonstration of God's omnipotent goodness: the former because it would not exist but for sin; the latter because it shows how God can produce relative harmony, even out of disorder, by creating a structured system out of the diversities of creaturely wills and motivations. Moreover, he argues, this same physical world becomes the instrument of God for restoring his creatures to their original blessedness: in a word, the means of their education.

Thus, Origen writes:

> God . . . in providing for the salvation of his entire creation . . . has so ordered everything that each spirit or soul . . . should not be compelled by force against its free choice to any action except that to which the motions of its own mind lead it . . . and at the same time that the motions of their wills should work suitably and usefully together to produce the harmony of a single world, some being in need of help, others able to give help, others again to provide struggles and conflicts for those who are making progress.[17]

If the embodiment of spirits is the inevitable result of their loss of that unity and equality for which God created them, it is also the occasion for God's manifestation of his goodness and benevolence in the creation of an order which is harmonious in its own way, and which serves the ends of redemption.

The world, then, as Origen sees it, is essentially an order of rational spirits. Its physical articulation is determined by the varying qualities of their wills and minds; and its history is the pattern traced out by the course of their fall away from God and their restoration to the original state of unity with God from which they have defected. In this scheme, "matter" is not an independent principle of disorder, as it is for the followers of Plato or for the Gnostics. It is rather the logical product of the spirits' movement away from God. To degrees of sin, there correspond degrees of corporeity. This means that "matter" is, so to speak, the name of the limit toward which the soul moves as it retreats from God. To be embodied is indeed, then, to be subjected to futility, as St. Paul says. But morally speaking, this futility is not of matter's—or of God's—making. It is the just and inevitable consequence of the soul's defection from God.

In this way, Origen contrives to talk for practical purposes as a Platonist without actually espousing a Platonist system of the classical sort. As befits a student of the Scriptures, he is formally a monist and not a dualist. For him, there is only one ultimate "principle" of the world-order, and that is God. It is from the goodness of God that creaturely freedom derives; and under God, it is to creaturely freedom that the world owes its present shape. When, therefore, Origen divides existence into the two realms of Being and Becoming, he is not naming two correlative and independent factors in the make-up of the world. He is naming the two "directions" in which the soul may move: a positive, and a negative. It may move toward God, the source of its being, the invisible and intelligible truth; or it may tend away from God, progressively dissipating unity into multiplicity, order into disharmony, truth into error. In either case, the conditions of its existence—that is, the character of the world—are determined by the quality of its choice. If, then, there is a dualism in this picture of the world, it must, in principle at least, be sought in the nature of the soul itself: in the ambiguous character of its relation to God, as generate on the one hand, and as rational spirit on the other. Let us look, then, at Origen's delineation of the relation between soul and God, for this will carry us a step further in understanding of his outlook.

CREATURELY INTELLIGENCES

In this connection, our first step must be to clarify, as far as is possible, what Origen in fact understands by "creation," and what it means for him to say that something is "created." We have already seen that he accepts what by his time was the traditional Christian view that creation means generation "out of nothing." In the act of founding the world, God is absolute in his power. There is no external factor or condition which limits his purposes; and whatever he produces is therefore simply the expression of his own unconstrained goodness. As far as Origen is concerned, this doctrine is to be numbered among the *data* of Christian faith. He includes it in his summary of the Rule of Faith: "God is one, who created and set in order all things, and who, when nothing existed, caused the universe to be." [18]

The world of rational spirits, then, is created or generate *in this sense*. "All souls and all rational natures, whether holy or wicked, were made or created. All these are incorporeal in respect of their proper nature, but though incorporeal they were nevertheless made." [19] The interesting thing to note in this affirmation is that Origen feels it necessary to insist explicitly on the teaching that nonmaterial beings (or rather, *some* nonmaterial beings) must be classified as "created." He sees a difficulty in this doctrine, and it should not be hard, by this time, to grasp what the difficulty is. From the point of view of a Platonist, there is a contradiction involved in saying both that something is incorporeal and that it is generate. For this amounts to saying that it is both immaterial and material, that it belongs at once to the order of Being and to that of Becoming. But this is, in a sense, exactly what Origen wants to assert. The class of rational spirits, he thinks, must be generate—not only because that is what is meant by calling them created but also, as we have seen, because that is what explains their moral instability and hence their tendency to move away from God. On the other hand, they are not physical things, but incorporeal minds; for this fact is what accounts for their affinity with the divine Nature and their consequent tendency to seek God. Philosophically speaking, Origen wants to have his cake and eat it: and he must therefore take some care to explain what precisely he means when he calls incorporeal beings "generate" or "created."

The first thing he means is that these creatures have a "beginning." This is a perfectly respectable sense of the word "generate." Indeed, it is one sense of the term which explains why Christians more or less adopted it as a synonym for "made" or "created." But as we have seen in the cases of Justin, Irenaeus, and Tertullian, they ordinarily took it to mean a *temporal* beginning. Origen, however, is equivocal on this point. He records the traditional view: "The Church teaching . . . includes the doctrine that this world was made and *began to exist at a definite time*." [20] But he takes it that this doctrine applies to the world *in its present form*: to that articulated visible order which, as we have seen, is a product of the rational creatures' sin. For he goes on to indicate that this teaching does not answer all questions: "what existed before this world, or what will exist after it, has not yet been made known openly to the many, for no clear statement on the point is set forth in the Church teaching." [21] Of course, we already know at least part of Origen's answers to these further questions. What existed before this world was the order of rational spirits which God originally created. What is to be said, then, about their "beginning"?

It seems fairly clear—though disagreement exists on this point among interpreters of Origen—that he would prefer *not* to say that their beginning is temporal. He explains, in the treatise *On First Principles* as elsewhere, that there are more senses than one of the word "beginning." There is, he writes, a beginning which is "of that kind which can be distinguished by periods of time"; and another sort "which the mind alone is wont to contemplate in itself and to perceive . . . with the bare intellect and reason." [22] To say, therefore, that rational creatures have a "beginning" does not entail thinking that they have a temporal origin. It may signify simply that their existence is of the sort which is not self-explanatory—that to understand them, one must see them as dependent upon God both for their being and for their being what they are. And this, apparently, is just what Origen tends to think. He argues that the world—that is, the rational spirits—must in some form have existed eternally. Otherwise, he points out, it hardly makes sense to speak of God's forever exercising his power through his eternally begotten Word. "We can . . . imagine no moment whatever when that power was not engaged in acts of well-doing. Whence it follows that there always existed objects for this well-doing, namely, God's works or creatures." [23] The sense, therefore, in which the rational spirits have a "beginning" is *not* one which is inconsistent with their being eternal spiritual natures—as Plato had taught.

To be a creature, then, is to be "originate," and in this sense generate. But this implies, as we have seen, something further about the character or nature of the creatures. It suggests that they must be regarded as in themselves incomplete—eternally unfinished as they are eternally created. It is this incompleteness or imperfection which explains how they can be, as it were, retrograde, how they can have a "built-in" tendency to move in the direction of unreality and falsehood and, therefore, how a material universe can come into existence.

Here, then, is our answer to the question what Origen means by calling the world "generate" or "created." He means both that the rational spirits are originate and that they have the instability of nature which necessarily accompanies such a condition. But he will not allow that this instability extends to their very existence. By the will of their Creator, they are incorruptible; and Origen obviously prefers to think that, just as their existence can have no end, so it had no (temporal) beginning. And these two facets of his creation doctrine more or less exactly express his estimate of the character of the rational spirits. In their eternity and rationality, they are akin to God himself. In him, they have not only their source but also their end; and the knowledge of God is the fulfillment of their nature. But at the same time, even as members of a spiritual order, they are weak and imperfect because created. Their affinity for God is balanced by a drift toward nonbeing; their capacity to share in the perfect integrity of the One is accompanied by a tendency to relax, as it were, into a state of disintegration.

Needless to say, there is a question whether this account does not, in the end, raise as many problems as it solves. How, for example, is the radical instability of the rational spirits to be reconciled with Origen's obvious conviction that it is their affinity for God, for intelligible truth, which will prevail in the end? Origen has no clear answer for this question, though he was aware of it and wrestled with it.

But for our purposes, the very existence of this problem is illuminating because it reveals the essential logic of Origen's world-picture. In his eyes, the world is to be understood as the product of two "movements": a descending movement in which being is diffused and diversified, and an ascending movement by which it is integrated again with its source. Origen's problem (and the Neoplatonic philosopher Plotinus was to deal with it more successfully) is that of the reconciliation of these two tendencies. But the pattern of his thought remains in the face of the difficulty which it creates; and it is this pattern, which we have seen in his doctrines of the soul and of creation, which also governs his understanding of God and the Logos.

BEGINNING AND END

For Origen's God is the presupposition of both of these tendencies. In the treatise *On First Principles,* he portrays God in terms directly reminiscent of Middle Platonist theology, but with a difference. "God," he writes, "must not be thought to be any kind of body, nor to exist in a body, but to be a simple intellectual existence, admitting in himself of no addition whatever, so that he cannot be believed to have in himself a more or a less, but is Unity, or if I may so say, Oneness throughout, the mind and fount from which originates all intellectual existence or mind." [24] Just as matter, or Becoming, is the expression of diversity and multiplicity, so God is simple Unity, and therefore absolutely immaterial. At the same time, he is wholly without parts, and for this reason is exempt from the categories of space and time. In consequence, God transcends the world as the Source of all being and of all intelligence. He himself, as Origen explains, is "beyond being":[25] *"God does not even participate in being.* For he is participated in, rather than participates." [26] In other words, God is the Source, the timeless point of origin of whatever can be said to "be"; and it is therefore impossible to think of him adequately in terms of any of the descriptions which would apply to that which flows from him as its Source. In this consists his uniqueness and his transcendence.

In this account, there are two points to be noticed. The first is that God, as Origen portrays him, fulfills the role of the Platonist First God. He is the supreme Reality, truth itself and goodness itself. As such, it is he who is dimly known in the mind's search for a stable and intelligible reason of things. He is the light to which all created intelligences are drawn by their very need of truth. Simply by being what he is, therefore, God functions as the initiator of that movement by which all creatures tend to return to their original harmony and unity in the contemplation of truth.

On the other hand, in a fashion not at all typical of the sort of Platonism represented by Albinus, Origen's God is a subject of creative activity. His goodness expresses itself: it overflows in the generation of a world in which the divine perfection is mirrored in the harmony of an order of rational spirits. So central is this idea to Origen's conception of God that he insists, as we have seen, on the fact that one cannot think of God without thinking at the same time of the world in which God's creative goodness is manifested. The doctrine of "eternal creation" is, in Origen, a correlate of his understanding of the divine nature. It belongs to the idea of the Godhead that it is the timeless point of origin of a descending, and progressively diversifying, stream of existence. In his character as Truth, God is the source of that movement in the world by which all things return to their origin. In his essential creativity, God is the explanation of that movement by which being is articulated and multiplied at the level of creaturely existence.

And into this scheme, Origen fits the Logos-Word of the theology which he had inherited from his Christian predecessors. For the Logos appears in Origen's system as the first step "down" from the One in the stream of existence: the divine power in whom the perfection of the Godhead is perfectly set forth, but set forth in such wise that the reality of God is made articulate and comprehensible. Thus, Origen describes the Logos as the personally existing Will of God, the expression of the eternal Mind. "As an act of will proceeds from the mind without either cutting off any part of the mind or separated or divided from it, in some similar fashion has the Father begotten the Son." [27] The Logos is therefore the immediate product of the Father, the direct manifestation of his being. As such, he is, of course, "generated"—but not (as Justin and Tertullian seem to have taught) at some point prior to the creation of the world. The Logos is the eternal self-expression of God. He does not come into existence, nor is he susceptible of change.

Yet, Origen is quite clear about the fact that the Logos is

in some sense "less" than God. This is manifest in part from the role which is assigned him. Though "there is absolutely no dissimilarity between the Son and the Father," [28] yet the Word is a "second God," [29] the brightness which streams from the eternal light. He transcends and illuminates the rational spirits, just as he himself is transcended and illuminated by the Father.[30] By the same token, Origen can say that although the Son or Word is properly called "God," the Father, in relation to him, is called "Deity itself": *autotheos*.[31] Much the same point is made in the *Commentary on Matthew*, where Origen explains that the Father is the goodness of which the Word is the image.[32] The idea in all these frequently cited passages is fundamentally the same. Whatever the Father is, the Word is—but in a different way or at a different level. The Son stands between the supreme God and the world, articulating the divine nature in such a way that its power and grace can be made known in and for a creation which is diverse and multiple. In this fashion, the Logos takes his place as the first step below the One in the diffusion and diversification of Being. He is the first expression of that abundant creativity by which God eternally moves out of solitude; and he is the perfect expression, at the same time, of the unity with God toward which the whole creation moves. He is the eternal reconciliation of the two movements of diversification and of return to Unity; and Origen's view of the Logos can only fully be appreciated when it is seen that both of these elements are essential to it.

In a sense, therefore, Origen's doctrine of the Logos provides the focal point of his theological world-picture. At once in his unity with the Father and in his distinction from the Father, he is the exemplar and the pattern for all created intelligences. Participation in the Son's unity with the Father is the goal toward which the creation is meant to move. And in the light of this ideal, as it is spelled out in Origen's understanding of the nature of man, one can grasp clearly the differences of emphasis and of doctrine which distinguish his position from those of

Irenaeus and Tertullian. In such a scheme, there can be little room for an interest in the redemption of the physical component in the human constitution, or for a concern with the concrete course of history as the context of man's encounter with God. What Origen concentrates on is the ascent of the rational spirit to a sharing in that eternal Wisdom which is the very image of the divine nature.

And Origen's world-picture had the advantage, in his time, of suggesting a way by which the language of earlier theology could be given a clear and self-consistent philosophical sense. In this fact lay its essential superiority to the other theological proposals of this period in the Church's history. Its weakness lay in the fact that it only managed to make sense of the axioms of traditional Christian theology by introducing ideas which most believers either could not understand or could not accept. Origen as a matter of fact did not so much develop the themes of earlier theology as insert them into a context of thought which, although it succeeded in giving them a clear meaning, did not in most cases give them their obvious meaning. And the final judgment of Christian history on Origen's ideas might be summed up in the observation that they appeared too clever by far. But at the same time, they raised questions and created problems of such depth and scope that they defined the *problématique* of later theology. Origen's cleverness was not in vain.

Notes to Chapter V

1. *Against Celsus* VII.42. Here and elsewhere I have used Chadwick's translation of the *Contra Celsum*.
2. *On First Principles* I.3.1. All citations of this work are from Butterworth's translation.
3. *Ibid.* II.11.3.
4. *Ibid.*, *Praef.* 8.
5. *Against Celsus* VI.20; cf. *On First Principles* I.7.5; III.6.7.
6. *Ibid.* VII.46.
7. *Ibid.* VII.50.
8. *On First Principles* II.9.6.
9. *Against Celsus* IV.66 (italics mine).
10. *On First Principles* II.9.6.
11. *Ibid.* II.9.2.
12. *Ibid.*
13. *Ibid.*
14. *Ibid.*
15. *Ibid.*
16. *On First Principles* II.1.4.
17. *Ibid.* II.1.2.
18. *Ibid.*, *Praef.* 4.
19. *Ibid.* I.7.1.
20. *Ibid*, *Praef.* 7 (italics mine).
21. *Ibid.*
22. *Ibid.* I.2.2.
23. *Ibid.* I.4.3.
24. *Ibid.* I.1.6.
25. *Commentary on John* XIX.6.
26. *Against Celsus* VI.64.
27. *On First Principles* I.2.6.
28. *Ibid.* I.2.12.
29. E.g., *Against Celsus* V.39.
30. *Commentary on John* XIII.25.
31. *Commentary on John* II.2.
32. *Commentary on Matthew* XV.2.

CHAPTER VI. *The Achievement of the Fathers*

WE HAVE now surveyed the views of four representative Christian writers of the second and third centuries on certain crucial questions which were involved in the development of a Christian philosophical world-picture. In doing so, we have emphasized the ways in which these writers used and criticized the materials of the Greek philosophical tradition. Indeed, we have suggested, if only indirectly, that it was the resources and the challenge provided by Greek religious philosophy which at once enabled and compelled Christian ventures into the field of rational theology. It remains for us to inquire what can be said in a general and summary way about the character of this dialogue as we have observed it, and the theological fruit which it bore.

First of all, however, we must call attention to the complexity of the relation between Christian theology and Greek, or Hellenistic, thought generally. Because of the nature of our particular inquiry, we have perforce focused our interest on Christian use of certain philosophical ideas or themes—ideas drawn for the most part from the intellectual cadre of late Platonism, and ideas which functioned, or could function, in the development of a rational theology. But in following this course, we have run a double risk of oversimplification. For one thing, it must be noted that the development of a rational theology was only one—and that certainly not the most prominent—phenomenon in the life of the early Church. The Christian community had other interests, activities, and problems which brought it into dialogue with other sectors and other forms of Hellenistic intellectual and cultural life.

But this is not all. The more or less conscious dialogue with Greek philosophical theology on which we have concentrated here presupposes at every point a more primitive, and for that reason less critical, Christian appropriation of Greek ways of thinking. The very possibility of this dialogue can only be understood if we recognize the significance of the fact that even before it commenced, Christians were writing, reading their Scriptures, and doing their thinking *in Greek,* a language whose religious idiom was partly shaped in the context of philosophical speculation and belief. Quite naturally, therefore, they tended to understand and use the language of their own tradition in a way which reflected an unconscious appreciation of its "secular" employments and connotations. Hence, the Christianity which, in such a writer as Justin Martyr, one sees in dialogue with the dogmas of Greek philosophical religion is a Christianity which is already a naturalized citizen of the Hellenistic thought world.

It is in the light of this fact that one must understand the attitude of the writers we have studied toward Greek philosophy. In their own minds, they were essentially critics of Greek philosophy, as they were of traditional Greek religion. To be sure, their expressed feelings on this score varied significantly. One searches in vain in Justin for a trace of Tertullian's bitterness in condemning philosophy; and one seeks in vain in Irenaeus for Origen's practical "liberalism" of outlook. But to some extent these differences are the product of varying temperament, background, and education in the writers in question. In their formally stated teaching on the subject of Greek philosophy, their positions were remarkably similar; and in every case, the point of their teaching was the same. Human speculation, they thought, is an unreliable guide to follow in questions which concern the knowledge of God and the ultimate destiny of man. In these matters, the truth must ultimately be sought in the Scriptures. For the Scriptures teach a clear doctrine, whereas philosophy can offer only a mass of conflicting opinions; and at the same time, they teach a doctrine which is demonstrably different from the deliverances of any of the Greek schools of thought, including Platonism. In the first instance, the theological teaching of the early Fathers is the expression of a conscious criticism and rejection of Greek wisdom—of its method and outlook in particular, but also of its specific beliefs on certain subjects.

Yet these same writers believed and admitted that there were similarities and correspondences between the teaching of the Scriptures and that of the philosophers, especially, perhaps, that of the Platonists. And this admission, as they themselves saw, had to be explained if it were not to seem inconsistent with their over-all attitude. Consequently, they took pains to indicate why such agreements occurred and how they should be evaluated. The Greek thinkers, they explained, had "borrowed" many of their ideas from Scripture. And such truths as they had not in this way taken over—and distorted—from God's revelation of himself in the Bible were no more than developed "common notions," the universal sowings (as Justin would have it) of the spermatic Logos. In other words, the Fathers believed that the philosophical ideas whose validity, or partial validity, they were prepared to acknowledge were, in fact, either universal commonplaces of theological and moral discourse, or else elements in God's direct revelation of himself. In either case, these ideas would be found to inform the teaching of the Jewish Scriptures and the writings of the Apostles. For this reason, there could, in the minds of the Fathers, be little consciousness of "making use" of Greek ideas. If they did make use of Greek ideas—and to the modern reader of their works, it seems apparent that they did—it was with the conviction that they were appealing to the *data* of God's self-revelation, whether "general" or "special."

Here, then, is an explanation of the apparent ambiguity in

the attitude of the early Fathers toward Greek philosophical theology. If they "used" its resources, it was with the assurance that they were making appeal to certain principles of biblical teaching. If they criticized it, it was because they perceived that its deliverances were in one way or another contrary to the outlook of the Bible. In short, they went to work theologically on the assumption that Christian belief as set forth in the sources of revelation was *logically comparable* to the systems of pagan philosophy: that the two bodies of teaching were talking roughly the same language about the same essential issues, and thus, inevitably, shared certain common and elementary presuppositions. They believed, in a word, that the Scriptures supplied logically appropriate answers to the basic problems of Greek theological speculation; and on the basis of this not unimportant assumption, they proceeded to criticize and revise the teaching of their philosophical masters.

The ultimate, if not the immediate, result of their work was anything but insignificant, even philosophically. This was not because the Fathers were, for the most part, either vastly learned or remarkably clever as philosophers. But their bold, and not always perceptive, exposition of Christian teaching in terms of a Greek philosophical world-picture effected not merely a partial Hellenization of Christian thought but also a Christianization of Greek thought, the result of which was a transformation of Western philosophy. Their use of the terminology of the philosophical tradition to express thoughts and beliefs which were not native to it brought about a fruitful alteration in the very meaning of crucial philosophical symbols, and in this way created not merely a "new look" philosophically but also a new set of philosophical problems.

This general observation goes far toward indicating an answer to our more specific question about the theological fruit of the Fathers' dialogue with Greek philosophy. Their theology did not come to them ready-made; and the result of their labors was not a perfectly uniform point of view. There were, as we have seen, vast differences of outlook among Irenaeus, Tertullian, and Origen. It is true that they had certain clear principles in common. On such basic issues as the unity and transcendence of God, the doctrine of creation, the idea of the Logos, and the problem of evil, they exhibit a remarkable unanimity. One might reasonably assume, therefore, that these common principles represent the elementary axioms of a philosophical world-picture revised to fit the requirements of Christian faith.

But such a conclusion, although essentially correct, must nevertheless be qualified carefully. For it is also true that the meaning of these axioms depended to a certain extent on the way in which they were understood and interpreted. And at this level, wide variations of outlook were possible. In the writings of the Fathers, each of these principles stood for the affirmation of a theme of biblical faith, but in a philosophical idiom whose natural logic was not always consonant with that of the teaching it was used to express. Consequently, each of these principles turned out to be inherently *problematic*. Each was not only a *datum* for Christian belief but was also a focus for disagreement, discussion, and doctrinal development. How this was so can be seen more clearly if we review several of the central questions which early Christian thought was compelled to canvass.

1. The first and most basic issue with which the Fathers were concerned was that of the nature of God in his relation with the world. On this subject, they were the defenders and proponents of a party line. They had inherited the monotheism of the Jews, and with it a hostile attitude toward the teaching of popular Greek religion and philosophy. They were bound to assert their distinctive tenet that there is but one God and that this God is the single Lord of all the world. This meant not merely that they rejected polytheism in its more blatant forms but also that they were critical of any philosophical doctrine which envisaged the Divine as one among several correlative factors which account for the character of the world. For such a doctrine made

of God not the unique and transcendent Lord, but simply the most divine among the forces which determine the natural order, or the divine "sector" of the natural order itself.

But in order to explain their doctrine, Christian writers seized, as we have seen, on the Platonist distinction between Being and Becoming, invisible and visible existence. They identified God with Being—or sometimes, more subtly, with the Source of Being—and described him as immaterial, impassible, and ingenerate Mind. The reasons for this procedure we have already indicated. It was the Platonist tradition alone which, in its developed form, knew a God whose very nature set him beyond the world, and made him supreme over it as the origin of its rational order. It was therefore the Platonist tradition alone which provided a language naturally adapted to express the majesty, the mysteriousness, and the absoluteness of the biblical Lord. Yet the use of this language brought problems in its train.

For one thing, as we have seen in the case of Justin, it tended to suggest a picture of God as segregated from the world: a most puzzling definition of divine transcendence from a Christian point of view. By the same token, and quite consistently with this idea of transcendence, it envisaged God not as the subject of action within the world, but as the unchanging Object of man's intellectual and religious search for a stable reality. Many Christian writers, Justin apparently among them, simply juxtaposed these contrary conceptions of God. On the other hand, it is impossible not to recognize, in Irenaeus's polemic against Gnosis, a conscious attempt to fuse the idea of God as incorruptible Being with the doctrine that God is unlimited creative Power, intimately present *in* the finite world without in any sense being a part *of* it. In a different way, the same conceptions are fused by Origen, who pictures God not merely as the Object to which all intelligences are drawn but also as the creative Source of finite mind. One result, then, of the dialogue of Christian faith with Greek philosophy was the formulation of an idea of God which, at its very center, embraced a fundamental tension between the ideals of an immutable Perfection beyond the world and a creative Sovereignty in and over it.

2. It is in the context of this tension that we must understand early patristic treatments of the idea of the Logos. This must be counted among the common themes of Christian theology, and it bore directly on the problem of the relation between God and the world. Like the Christian idea of God itself, the doctrine of the Logos had its roots in the language of Scripture as well as in the theology of late Judaism, in which the figures of God's Word and God's Wisdom played a prominent role. But here, too, as Justin's treatment of the theme indicates clearly enough, Greek ideas had a determining influence. When Christian thinkers talked about the Logos, they tended to have in their minds the analogy of the late Platonist World Soul: the Cosmic Mind, or Reason, whose knowledge of the supreme God was the source of order and harmony in the visible world. It was by the use of this conception of a mediating divine Reason that Justin, for example, explained the relation of the transcendent and ingenerate God to the world of generate existence. The Logos was the instrumental means through whom God created the world, revealed himself, and redeemed mankind.

But this set of associations, like the identification of God with Being, created a number of problems, with which the writers whom we have studied were compelled, in one way or another, to come to terms. Most obviously, perhaps, it raised the question of the relation of the Logos to God—which, in a Christian system, with its insistence on the unity and uniqueness of God, was indeed a serious issue. At the same time, it tended to accentuate, by the interposition of a "generate God," the isolation of God as Being from the world as Becoming.

For Irenaeus, both of these problems were raised in an acute form as a result of his efforts to counter the logic of Gnostic cosmology. In the light of his strictures on the Gnostic system of Eons, Irenaeus found the idea of a mediating Deity thoroughly embarrassing, just as he did the idea of a God who is somehow segregated from the visible world. Consequently, he shows a tendency to treat the Word (and the Spirit) not as slightly inferior divinities, but simply as substantive modes of God's active presence in and for the world. Origen, on the other hand, deals with the problem in a way which reflects his more exact appreciation of the philosophical presuppositions of the Logos doctrine. He integrates the Logos into his scheme of a hierarchy of being governed by the contrary tendencies of descent from, and return to, Unity. In this scheme, the Logos fits perfectly, as the eternal manifestation of the reconciliation of these two movements. Unchangeably one with God, the Word nevertheless articulates the Godhead in such a way as to be both the Wisdom which finite spirits can grasp and the Guide who restores them to that unity with God which is his by nature. This explanation differs widely from Irenaeus's. Yet both authors are explaining and interpreting the same traditional theme of Christian theology.

It should be plain that the problem with which they—and Tertullian with his idea of a differentiated divine "substance"— are dealing is precisely the product of an attempt to assimilate Christian teaching to a Platonist world-picture. The question of the nature of the Logos, which was to come to a head in the Arian controversies of the fourth century, stems from the association of the Word of God with the immanent World Soul; and it was further complicated by the characterization of the Logos as "generate," with all that that term connoted philosophically in the way of inferiority of status. As in the case of the doctrine of God, the history of Christian speculation about the Logos is in part the story of an attempt to qualify or to overcome certain implications of the philosophical ideas which were first used to give rational expression to the Church's belief, and which were never wholly repudiated.

3. The same pattern, finally, is discernible in early Christian discussions of the related questions of the character of the finite world, the origin of evil, and the destiny of man. The tensions in Christian thought about these issues result directly from

the conflict between the idea of the world as the realm of Becoming and the doctrine that the world is the creation of God. These two conceptions, as we have seen, were used more or less as equivalents. To describe the world as "generate" was regarded, in Christian circles, as meaning that it is the product of the almighty divine will. Yet these "equivalents" seemed to have contrary contextual implications, and for the good reason that they derived from different frameworks of thought.

What did it mean to describe the world and God as generate and ingenerate respectively? First, it inevitably suggested an *evaluation* of the spatiotemporal order as the realm of change, relative disorder, and irrationality. Second, it called to mind the idea that evil arises out of the rational soul's involvement in this order—out of its embodiment or, more subtly, out of its created and therefore finite character. Finally, it indicated that man's salvation lies in the overcoming of this involvement in the generate order, and in the realization of his intellectual nature through knowledge of God.

On the other hand—as every Christian writer of this period was, to one degree or another, aware—the doctrine that the world is God's creation "out of nothing" contradicts these ideas at several points. For one thing, it must refuse to admit that matter, now regarded perforce as the creature of God, can be by nature alien from its Creator; and this refusal was lent further support by the doctrine of a bodily resurrection. By the same token, Christians saw clearly that their idea of creation demanded that the soul itself be included in the class of "generate" beings. And because the work of God is surely good in its essential character, this doctrine was bound to find the source of evil, as Origen so clearly recognized, in the freedom of created wills, and not in any set of conditions to which the soul is subjected.

There is nothing more baffling in the thought of the Church Fathers than the variety of ways in which they combine, or seek consciously to reconcile, these two sets of apparently contrary ideas about the world, its relation to God, and man's destiny within it. Origen is an obvious case in point. From one point of view, his account of the creation can be seen as a careful defense of certain biblical themes—the goodness of the finite order, the definition of evil as *sin*—against the criticisms of Gnostic and Platonist thinkers. On the other hand, Origen contrives to expound these themes in such a way that a Platonist evaluation of materiality and a Platonist idea of man's nature and destiny as rational spirit are enshrined as parts of the very substance of a Christian world-view.

Or take the case of Irenaeus. It need hardly be said that his outlook differs from Origen's not merely in points of detail but in its whole spirit. Yet in Irenaeus, too, one can perceive the mingling of these two divergent estimates of the world and of man. He is, of course, emphatic in his rejection of any notion that man's physical nature is alien to God. Nothing is more typical of him than his insistence that the body itself, through the work of Christ, can come to share in an incorruptible kind of existence. But at the same time, he points to the "generate" nature of man to explain the possibility of evil, and he accepts, for soul and body alike, a Platonizing ideal of redemption as a sharing in the characteristics of ingenerate existence. Equally symptomatic is his use of the Platonist idea of the contemplative vision of God to define the goal of the soul's pilgrimage.

But in all these cases, what we observe is not a surrender of Christianity to Hellenism, nor the reverse of this, but a fusion of ideas and themes which creates a new set of philosophical and theological problems, and thus lays the foundation for the working out, by future thinkers, of a new and necessarily more subtle understanding of man and his world in their relation to God.

Modern students of the Fathers, observing the way in which they appropriated something of the language, the ideas, and the ideals of Greek thought, have reacted to this phenomenon in widely differing ways. Some have seen in it a conscious or unconscious betrayal of the very substance of the Church's Gospel. Others, taking a more apologetic stance, have sought to defend the Fathers against this charge by minimizing the degree or the significance of Greek influence on their thought. Still others have appealed to patristic theology as a laudable example of a thoroughgoing assimilation of Christian teaching to the cultural forms of the world in which the Church is set.

None of these estimates, however, seems in the last analysis adequate to the facts. Christianity did address itself to the problems of rational theology in the Greek tradition, and in doing so it did take over the thought forms of Greek philosophy. But this procedure did not grow out of a conviction that Christian belief either could in fact be shown, or should in principle be shown, to have the same essential content as popular Greek religious philosophy. On the contrary, it grew out of an attempt to state an adequate—that is, distinctively scriptural—account of God and the world, and to do so in the philosophical language which was the natural and necessary vehicle of any theological enterprise in the Roman-Hellenistic world.

It turned out, of course, that biblical principles and philosophical terminology did not always march comfortably in step. They tended, as it were, to pull in different logical directions; and their divergent tendencies had again and again to be restrained, reconciled, and mutually adjusted. But it is their acceptance of the necessity for such a process of continual dialectical adjustment which accounts for the intellectual fertility of the Fathers' achievement. The fruit of their work was not the canonization of a Hellenistic Platonism or Stoicism. It was rather a sort of map of the problems involved in the elaboration of something which had never existed before: a biblical philosophy.

In the last resort, then, the theological legacy of the early Fathers was not a settled system, but a series of interrelated problematic themes. It left room for disagreement, for evolution, and for refinement. At the same time, however, the character of the problems themselves defined a direction of thought. They could only be understood in terms of the philosophical and religious presuppositions which gave them meaning and point.

Therefore, to enter into the theology of the Fathers means both to step into a debate and at the same time to share with them a set of interests and assumptions which provide the outlines of a world-picture even though they do not amount to a finished theological system. The early Church in fact failed—or refused —to make a perfect adjustment to the thought forms of the culture in which it existed; and the intellectual imbalance which it thus achieved was salutary in at least one respect. It was a guarantee of flexibility, as well as the seed of future creative development.

Bibliography

General Works

There are a number of books, older and more recent, in which the reader will find introductory studies of the early development of Christian theology. The classic work, now outdated but always stimulating, is A. von Harnack's *History of Dogma,* now available in a paper edition (New York: Dover, 1960). The second volume is pertinent to the period covered by this book. More concise, and at the same time more detailed and up-to-date, is J. N. D. Kelly's *Early Christian Doctrines* (New York: Harper & Bros., 1960). For historical and biographical detail, reference may be made to H. von Campenhausen, *The Fathers of the Greek Church* (New York: Pantheon Books, 1959); and *The Fathers of the Latin Church* (London: A. & C. Black, 1964); or to such works of reference as J. Quasten, *Patrology,* Vols. I and II (Westminster: Newman Press, 1950–53); and F. L. Cross, *The Early Christian Fathers* (London: Gerald Duckworth, 1960).

There is a considerable literature which deals in a general way with the relation between Greek and Christian thought in the second and third centuries. Among older works, still useful, are E. Hatch's Hibbert Lectures of 1888, *The Influence of Greek Ideas on Christianity* (New York: Harper Torchbooks, 1957); and T. R. Glover, *The Conflict of Religions in the Early Roman Empire* (Boston: Beacon Press, 1960). Particularly illuminating are A.-J. Festugière, *L'Idéal religieux des Grecs et l'Évangile* (Paris: J. Gabalda, 1932); and C. H. Dodd, *The Bible and the Greeks* (London: Hodder & Stoughton, 1954). Among more recent works, particular note should be taken of A. H. Armstrong and R. A. Markus, *Christian Faith and Greek Philosophy* (New York: Sheed & Ward, 1960); A. D. Nock, *Early Gentile Christianity and Its Hellenistic Background* (New York: Harper & Row, 1964); and of Jean Daniélou, *Message évangelique et culture hellenistique* (Tournai: Desclée et Cie., 1961). With these should be mentioned H. A. Wolfson, *The*

Philosophy of the Church Fathers, Vol. I (Cambridge, Mass.: Harvard University Press, 1956), which is concerned especially with the influence of Philo on the Church Fathers. Informative studies of particular issues may be found in G. L. Prestige, *God in Patristic Thought* (London: SPCK, 1952); R. M. Grant, *Miracle and Natural Law in Graeco-Roman and Early Christian Thought* (Amsterdam: North Holland Publishing Co., 1952); and W. Pannenberg, "Die Aufnahme des philosophischen Gottesbegriffs als dogmatisches Problem der frühchristlichen Theologie," in *Zeitschrift für Kirchengeschichte* (1959).

CHAPTER I: *Greek and Hellenistic Cosmology*

The literature relating to the history of Greek religion and religious philosophy is vast, and it is impossible here to give more than a bare sampling of certain standard works in English. The reader will, of course, wish to consult the works of M. P. Nilsson, *The History of Greek Religion* (Oxford: Clarendon Press, 1949); and *Greek Piety* (Oxford: Clarendon Press, 1948). For the history of Greek philosophy, there is the lucid work of A. H. Armstrong, *An Introduction to Ancient Philosophy* (London: Methuen & Co., 1957). In addition to these, he may read Gilbert Murray, *Five Stages of Greek Religion* (New York: Doubleday Anchor Books, 1955); and, more useful still, A.-J. Festugière, *Personal Religion among the Greeks* (Berkeley: University of California Press, 1954).

There are many introductions to Plato. A useful one is A. E. Taylor's *Plato: The Man and His Work,* which has the additional advantage of being available in paperback (New York: Meridian Books, 1957). An account of Plato's thought which is both more contemporary and more detailed will be found in the two volumes of I. M. Crombie's *Examination of Plato's Doctrines* (New York: Humanities Press, 1962–63). The best introduction to the *Timaeus* is probably F. M. Cornford's translation with commentary, *Plato's Cosmology* (London: Routledge and Kegan Paul, 1952), of which a paper edition is now available. The serious student should also consult A. E. Taylor's *Commentary on the Timaeus of Plato* (Oxford, Eng.: University Press, 1928).

For an introductory account of classical Stoicism, one can refer to E. R. Bevan's *Stoics and Sceptics* (latest reprint, Cambridge, Eng.: W. Heffer & Sons, 1959); and supplement it by consulting Diogenes Laertius's lives of Zeno and Cleanthes in the Loeb Library version of his *Lives of Eminent Philosophers* (Cambridge, Mass.: Harvard University Press, 1958). Equally useful are recent reprints of R. D. Hicks, *Stoic and Epi-*

curean (New York: Russell and Russell, 1962); and E. V. Arnold, *Roman Stoicism* (London: Routledge and Kegan Paul, 1958). On Middle Platonism, R. E. Witt, *Albinus and the History of Middle Platonism* (Cambridge, Eng.: University Press, 1937) should be consulted. There is a helpful collection of texts in E. R. Bevan, ed., *Later Greek Religion* (New York: E. P. Dutton, 1927).

CHAPTER II: *Justin Martyr and Platonism*

English versions (not always satisfactory) of the two apologies and the *Dialogue with Trypho* will be found in Volume I of *The Ante-Nicene Fathers* (Grand Rapids, Mich.: reprinted by W. B. Eerdmans, n.d.); and in Volume II of *The Ante-Nicene Christian Library* (Edinburgh: T. & T. Clark, 1870). A better version of the *First Apology* appears in Volume I of *The Library of Christian Classics* (Philadelphia: Westminster Press, 1953). The best introduction to Justin's thought is that of E. R. Goodenough, *The Theology of Justin Martyr* (Jena: Fromann, 1923). For Justin's relation to Middle Platonism, see the recent work of G. Andresen, "Justin und der mittlere Platonismus," in *Zeitschrift für die neutestamentlichen Wissenschaft*, XLIV (1952–53); and R. Holte, "Logos Spermatikos: Christianity and Ancient Philosophy according to St Justin's Apologies," in *Studia Theologica*, XII (1958).

CHAPTER III: *Irenaeus and the Gnostic Problem*

An English version of Irenaeus's treatise *Against Heresies* will be found in Volume I of *The Ante-Nicene Fathers* (Grand Rapids, Mich.: reprinted by W. B. Eerdmans, n.d.). Works in English on Irenaeus's theology include J. Lawson, *The Biblical Theology of Saint Irenaeus* (London: Epworth Press, 1948); and G. Wingren, *Man and The Incarnation* (Edinburgh and London: Oliver & Boyd, 1959). However, the best initiation to the work of Irenaeus is André Benoit, *Saint Irénée: Introduction à l'étude de sa théologie* (Paris: Presses Universitaires de France, 1960); and this should be supplemented by the work of A. Houssiau, *La Christologie de saint Irénée* (Louvain: Publications Universitaires de Louvain, 1955). Readers may also consult R. M. Grant, "Irenaeus and Hellenistic Culture," in *Harvard Theological Review*, XLII (1949); and M. Aubineau, "Incorruptibilité et divinisation selon saint Irénée," in *Recherches de Science Religieuse*, XLIV (1956).

On Irenaeus's account of Gnosticism, see F.-M.-M. Sagnard, O.P., *La Gnose Valentinienne et le témoignage de saint Irénée* (Paris: J. Vrin, 1947). For an old but helpful introduction to Gnosticism, the reader may use F. C. Burkitt, *Church and Gnosis* (Cambridge, Eng.: University Press, 1932). Among more recent studies, R. McL. Wilson, *The Gnostic Problem* (London: Mowbray, 1958); R. M. Grant, *Gnosticism and Early Christianity* (New York: Columbia University Press, 1959); and F. L. Cross, ed., *The Jung Codex* (London: Mowbray, 1955) are all suggestive. In *Gnosticism* (New York: Harper & Bros., 1961), R. M. Grant provides a collection of second-century Gnostic texts.

CHAPTER IV: *Tertullian—A Latin Perspective*

An English version of the works of Tertullian is available in both *The Ante-Nicene Fathers* (Grand Rapids, Mich.: W. B. Eerdmans, n.d.) and *The Ante-Nicene Christian Library* (Edinburgh: T. & T. Clark, 1870). Translations of individual treatises can be found in other series: e.g., *The Library of Christian Classics* (Vol. V: *Early Latin Theology*); and in various volumes of The Newman Press's series, *Ancient Christian Writers*.

For introductory studies of Tertullian as a man and a thinker, the reader may refer to P. de Labriolle, *History and Literature of Christianity from Tertullian to Boethius* (New York: Alfred A. Knopf, 1925); A. d'Alès, *La Théologie de Tertullien* (Paris: Beauchesne et Cie., 1905); and Roberts, *The Theology of Tertullian* (London: J. A. Sharp, 1924). R. Braun, *Deus Christianorum: Recherches sur le vocabulaire doctrinal de Tertullien* (Paris: Presses Universitaires de France, 1962), provides something of a conspectus of Tertullian's thought and takes into account recent detailed studies of Tertullian's language and style. Readers interested in Tertullian's doctrine of the Trinity should consult this work, together with E. Evans's introduction to the treatise *Against Praxeas* (*Tertullian's Treatise Against Praxeas,* London: SPCK, 1948); and G. C. Stead, "Divine Substance in Tertullian," in *The Journal of Theological Studies,* n.s., XIV (1963).

CHAPTER V: *Origen—A New Christian Platonism*

The literature on Origen is immense. Readers who wish to study his treatise *On First Principles* in English may use the version in *The Ante-Nicene Fathers,* Vol. IV, which also contains a translation of the work *Against Celsus.* They would do better, however, to procure, if they can, a copy of G. W. Butterworth's *Origen on First Principles* (London: SPCK, 1936); and to use H. Chadwick's magisterial translation of the treatise *Against Celsus* (*Origen: Contra Celsum*; Cambridge, Eng.: University Press, 1953).

For an introduction to Origen's thought, there is C. Bigg's set of Bampton Lectures—outdated but still not without value—*Christian Platonists of Alexandria* (Oxford: H. Milford, 1913). The standard introduction now, however, is undoubtedly Jean Daniélou's *Origen* (New York: Sheed & Ward, 1955), which can be supplemented by E. Molland's *The Conception of the Gospel in Alexandrian Theology* (Oslo, 1939). On the relation between Origen and late Platonism, H. Koch, *Pronoia und Paideusis* (Berlin: De Gruyter, 1932), should be read together with H. Crouzel, *Origène et la philosophie* (Paris: Aubier, 1962); and E. von Ivanka, "Der geistige Ort von *Peri archon* zwischen dem Neuplatonismus, der Gnosis, und der christlichen Rechtgläubigkeit," in *Scholastik*, XXXV (1960). Origen's exegetical method is treated by R. P. C. Hanson in *Allegory and Event* (London: SCM Press, 1959); and this book, together with the same author's *Origen's Doctrine of Tradition* (London: SPCK, 1954), casts much light on the general question of Origen's theological method.

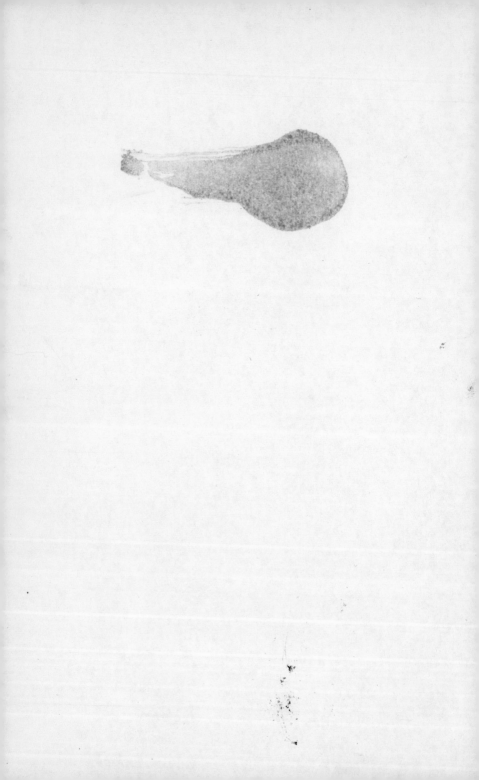